# Good Will & Ice Cream

# Good Will & Ice Cream
## More True Tales from Extraordinary Lives
## RICHIE DAVIS

painting by Rebecca B. Clark

**forty years of writing from *The Recorder*
of western Massachusetts**

Haley's

Athol, Massachusetts

Stories first appeared between 1976 and 2018 in *The Recorder* of Greenfield, Massachusetts and are used by permission of Newspapers of Massachusetts, Inc.

Copy edited by Debra Ellis.

Cover art, "Lake II" in soft pastels on Rives BFK paper by Rebecca B. Clark. Author photo on back cover by Lindy Whiton.

Haley's
488 South Main Street
Athol, MA 01331

International Standard Book Number 978-1-948380-68-3, trade paperback
International Standard Book Number 978-1-948380-43-0, ebook,
        watermarked pdf

Library of Congress Cataloguing in Publishing data pending

*for Susan*

*and*

*for David Kaynor*

Between words,
let there be
space     enough
for  living,
grace.


Beyond  words,
an  essence
true,  magic,
universe,
you.

—Richie Davis

# Contents

# Photographs

# Taking Time to Listen

## a foreword by BJ Roche

There's much hand-wringing these days about the decline of local news—the everyday accounting of events and actions by municipal government so important to the workings of democracy. The internet, social media, and changes in local retail have all contributed in one way or another to the slow death of that most valuable of resources, the local daily newspaper.

In the 1980s, four print and radio reporters covered weekly selectboard's meetings in the little town of Charlemont in western Franklin County, Massachusetts, for example. Today, there's no regular coverage at all, and people are more likely to get their news from Facebook than from "the paper."

I was one of those reporters, a correspondent for the *Recorder* of Greenfield.

Back then, I'd get up at 5:45 Thursday mornings to call in my story to Dolly Gagnon, the newspaper's typist. Then I'd put on some coffee and wait for my 6:30 phone call to go over the story with my editor, Richie Davis.

xiii

For years, Richie wrangled the contributions and massaged the copy of correspondents from the farflung towns of west county, the Orange-Athol area, Northfield, and Bernardston. By midday, he'd have woven together the collection of stories, meeting reports, and notebook items that would represent that day's edition of the *Recorder,* another contribution to the first draft of history in Franklin County.

As the collection of stories in this book attests, Richie is far more than a mentor and editor—he is also an elegant, empathic, and thoughtful writer whose deep knowledge of—and love for—the region and its people shines through in these stories. And in one way, the collection also represents a bit of history of Franklin County.

For when we talk about local news, we don't mean only taxes and school budgets. We're also talking about the landscapes, traditions, and people who create the texture of a community, its sense of place, the reasons you wouldn't live anywhere else. It should be noted that Franklin County—more rural, less hip than Amherst or Northampton, not as tony as the Berkshires—is not an easy place to nail down. With its mix of agriculture and old mill economies, Franklin County is among the poorest and whitest in the state. Not everyone loves the paper, which some occasionally disparage as the *Distorter.*

And it's not always easy getting, say, a Yankee dairy farmer in the outer reaches of Colrain to bare his soul. But Richie could do it, because he's a listener. That's a core skill for a local reporter, taking the time to listen to people who don't often have their say—getting it down and sharing it.

After years of all those early morning phone calls, Richie left the *Recorder* to work at a newspaper in Springfield for a while. Hey, the grass seemed greener.

But he came back. And wrote and wrote and wrote.

And readers are the richer for it.

In this collection, which spans more than forty years of writing, we meet town officials, storekeepers, peacemakers, and rabblerousers. There are dairy farmers and composers, a Tibetan stonemason, and a driver for the Dalai Lama. There are filmmakers and ice-cream makers and a persnickety public radio host. Some are locals, others "from away." Some, like filmmaker Ken Burns, musician Paul Winter, and counterculture journalist Ray Mungo are semi- or well-known. Most are not. What they all have in common is a life spent in or a visit to Franklin County. All had a story, and each told it to Richie.

Here now is the sixties-era tale—a legend, really—of the theft and transport of the Liberation News Service printing press in the dark of night from Manhattan by a bunch of hippie journalists to a farm in Montague as part of a back-to-the-land movement. One young local there named Sam Lovejoy felled a tower on the Montague Plains that turned out to be the opening salvo of the antinuclear movement. Lovejoy went on to become a town selectman. Franklin County is that kind of place.

And here, forty years later, we meet Ben Clark, a third-generation orchard farmer who experienced his personal back-to-the-land movement when he returned to his family's hundred-year-old apple orchard after years away in the city. Clark was part of a shift that has helped revitalize local agriculture in recent decades.

Farming is, of course, a theme in the region, and it's easy to romanticize. But Richie avoids that trap, and his story on the Allen family of Greenfield takes a clear-eyed look at the uphill challenges of small-dairy farming in the modern age. Belying what some describe as the region's rural and somewhat isolated nature, there's a strong love for the arts in Franklin County and sometimes surprising connections to the larger world. Many artists make their homes here or pass through, performing at summer festivals or fall venues. We meet several, including composer and musician David Amram, who seems to have worked with practically everybody. The occasion is the performance of a composition based on the works of Woody Guthrie performed in Northampton by the Pioneer Valley Symphony.

There are stories about how others have looked at the area, stories fascinating for their insights about the endurance of the landscape, smalltown traditions, and the people. What has changed, what remains the same? The answers can surprise.

In one story, Richie revisits the 1978 prize-winning documentary *Root Hog or Die,* which then-young filmmaker Rawn Fulton made in Franklin County in the mid 1970s. The film made a splash locally back then and remains one of the best verité accounts of New England hilltown farming ever created. As Richie writes, *Root Hog* holds up as a historical document of the hardships of hillside farming, but it's also testimony to the perseverance of the filmmaker himself in creating and completing the work. Another story examines, fifty years later, the production of a US government propaganda film about a group of European refugees and their impact when they arrived in the town of Cummington during World War II. Spoiler alert: It may have looked like a Rockwell painting, but it was not.

Interestingly enough for a smalltown reporter, war and peace—how we make it and how we keep it—is a theme in Richie's work. In *Our Common Denominator,* he puts himself into the story of a group of students from around the world studying peacebuilding at the School for International Training in Brattleboro, Vermont. The story shows how each individual has a history we can never know and that empathy can be as strong a weapon as a missile.

All those subjects come from Richie's own interests as a musician, optimist, and person of the world. There are a lot of terrible things about working as a smalltown journalist: the pay is lousy, your boss may be a son of a bitch, and some days, it seems like everyone just has a complaint about the paper.

But when it's fun, any reporter will tell you, there's no better way to make a living. Richie has had a lot of fun over the years, and I think you'll share his joy with this collection.

Now . . . get reading!

BJ Roche is a writer and teacher who lives in Franklin County. Over a twenty-five-year career, she worked for several small newspapers in western Massachusetts and covered the region for the Boston Globe and the Boston Globe Magazine. Now retired from the journalism faculty at UMass Amherst, she worked in the early 1980s as one of the Greenfield Recorder's team of correspondents overseen by Richie Davis when he served as the newspaper's county editor.

# Good Will & Ice Cream

## an introduction by Richie Davis

Imagine yourself behind the pages of a newspaper being produced. What might come to mind is the keyboard-pounding grit of the kind of big-city newsroom depicted in movie classics like *The Front Page* or maybe *All the President's Men*. Though it all seems downright prehistoric today, especially depending on how old you are.

Our hinterland newsroom with plenty of those industrial-strength 1950s typewriters when I arrived in 1976, had a quaint, waist-high swinging gate past which visitors meandered, bringing story tips eagerly, wedding or birth announcements joyfully, or obituaries somberly. And yes, sometimes complaints angrily.

Community journalism is a different, homier animal than the big-city variety, I discovered during my nearly forty-five years as a reporter and editor. Our give-and-take with folks played out all the time, whether we were out walking on Main Street or shopping at Foster's Supermarket, the go-to family-run destination for fresh fish and produce from around our 725-square-mile county in western Massachusetts.

The mom-and-pop grocery, started in 1941 by Bud Foster, remains a comfortable destination where folks from around Franklin County run into neighbors from around the community and carry on relaxed conversations amid cabbages or around the deli counter. So it never surprised me over decades reporting for the only newspaper in town to be stopped in one aisle or another by someone to critique a story I'd written.

"Hey, aren't you . . . ?"

Such is the price of "fame" in a small town, where it's hard to remain anonymous. The comments, nearly always complimentary, flowed freely, though often, the person couldn't recall which story they'd liked before our ice cream began melting. Sometimes, absolute strangers who recognized me from a photo printed beside my columns would approach to say, "You don't know who I am, but I just want to tell you how much I appreciate what you do."

"How could I be so lucky?" I'd ask myself, bearing in mind that I was also the target of my share of hate mail from readers. "How fortunate to get this kind of gratification. Why is it I get to have such a fascinating job that also connects me with so many people?"

At least when I wasn't being cursed for my work. Or when I'd have to conveniently remember a shopping-list item in another aisle to avoid someone I knew would always have a bone to pick with me.

Smalltown feedback seemed constant, often coming from surprising faces in odd places. Like the phone calls at home from readers asking a question about my story or for extra information they could have easily found in the phone book.

Or the kid next door when I saw him in the yard one day.

"Hey, do you work at the *Recorder*?"

"Yup, I do."

"Your TV listings are wrong all the time! How come they're wrong?"

At least the comics were right.

Was that the reward for writing for a small newspaper instead of a big metro? Is it because I opted out of journalism school and chose real-life learning? Maybe it's that I persisted in "doing my thing" rather than getting promoted away from pounding the keyboard?

For years, I was seemingly left behind as I watched fellow reporters leave for the big time or give up newspapering for what others considered a real job. But here I was not only covering courts and police, nuclear power and environmental issues, but also creating enterprising features that grounded me and mattered to a community I continue to feel a strong part of.

I felt lucky being able to write, for example, a series about recent immigrants from the former Soviet republics, about nuclear plants and planned gas lines, about spirituality, rural poverty, aging baby boomers, and even yogurt.

My imagination got a workout creating a series chronicling the yearlong startup of a restaurant from pipedream to destination bistro. I got to develop a trivia board game about our region and even a *Flights of Fancy* feature that toured the Massachusetts footsteps of Jack Kerouac, Mary's little lamb, Elsie the Cow, and Dr. Seuss.

But winning reporting awards and community honors like a Local Hero from agriculture advocates paled to the thrill of creating and exploring subjects in new ways and hearing from real people while grocery shopping—or simply walking along Main Street.

Clearly, I was lucky, I figured, but that bubble—which I always knew could burst at any moment was also about having coworkers willing to collaborate and support from editors and publishers dedicated to giving readers stories that touched and reflected the community.

It was also a community where people had an interest in learning about the creative genius, dedication, and hard work of folks around them. It also has had a strong sense of place distinct from any nearby metropolis.

But as much as being about our area, the good fortune I experienced was also about our era, when newspapers still had resources and stable readership. Or so it seemed.

Who could have imagined, when my first book of stories was about to be published in the spring of 2020, that a pandemic would engulf the planet, isolating people and destroying entire economies?

Newspapers were already suffering from internet competition over the past twenty to thirty years—with traditional revenue models upturned and reading habits swept away by free online, round-the-clock "news."

By the time I'd arrived in newsrooms in the mid-1970s—about a decade after "hot" lead type had given way to the "cold-type" photo offset revolution, with layoff of linotype operators and proofreaders–computers were redefining our world and TV was undermining reading habits.

Our afternoon newspaper gave way to a morning edition, and the race was on to cast ourselves as an all-day paper to pretend we were churning out stories around the clock.

But the appeal of "news from everywhere" instantly, anytime at the touch of a button—and free, no less—has devastated newspapers, and advertising dollars have been sucked up by social media platforms. Small papers, in particular, struggle to keep up with multitasking by publishing online plus print editions— a relentless press-like treadmill for reporters. No wonder quality and depth of reporting and writing often suffers.

As I pore over the articles in this book that mean so much to me, the more encompassing story looms large: the importance of community journalism.

The rigors of responsible reporting, shining light on truths that some would prefer to remain hidden, is essential for  our democracy.

And the stories that we're told, the examples of diverse lives lived around us, truly matter.

For me, as filmmaker Ken Burns described of his own work, "I want these to be honest, complicated portraits that are unafraid of controversy and tragedy, but also are drawn to the things that animate our souls."

My life has been enriched by immersing myself in community journalism and sharing the stories of people like David Kaynor and the Clarks, conveying the passions of Blanche Moyse, the courage of Waitstill and Martha Sharp, and the openheartedness of the Zen Peacemakers bearing witness at Auschwitz. And I glow knowing I've helped enrich the lives of those around me.

Our stories are what connect us as human beings. Beyond the passions that each person in this collection reveals, each of their stories exemplifies for me dozens in which I've tried to convey, beyond words, the meaning imbued by their lives.

I'm thrilled to share the stories and the people they represent so they can live on. If I've succeeded in conveying even a fraction of the wonder those lives speak to me, I'll feel a gratitude similar to what I was left with by connecting with those grocery shoppers.

The lives that touch our own often run deep. That's apparent if we can look beyond the words.

The stories here, originally published in the *Greenfield Recorder* between August 1976 and February 2018, cover a wide range of personalities and themes that appealed to me not only as a reporter, but also as someone immersed in our vibrant community—even though I've included subjects with much wider connections, such as David Amram, Ken Burns, and Robert J. Lurtsema.

My aim in this collection has been to include feature stories as they appeared in the newspaper. Yet in several instances when I've written over time multiple stories about various aspects of a single character, I've combined some of those stories together. Deb Habib, for example, has worked with teens and gotten people around the region to start planting gardens. Paula Green has planted her seeds of peace around the globe as well as around the nation.

Among my very favorite adventures were entire days spent with farmers like Gerry Allen in order to convey to readers how much tireless work goes into producing our food. Allen, whose story represents for me the constant struggle of dairy farmers to keep up with diminishing returns for their efforts, was a special treat because I decided to revisit him after several years to see how his optimism was holding up. In this collection, I've included part of the later visit in the same story.

When I'm presenting more than a single story here, I've noted it in the text. All of the stories have been re-edited, but for the most part, the situations are presented as they were at the time.

Because the conversations seemed then and still strike me as timeless, I've chosen most often to write in present tense rather than the strict journalistic "he said"/"she said" style. I apologize in advance for any confusion that choice may cause for the reader. For me, the characters here–even those who've long ago passed on–remain very much alive and present with their ideas and their ideals.

photo by Paul Franz

Ben Clark, left, and Tom Clark

# Rooted on the Farm

## January 6, 2011

*One of the most promising changes I observed over four decades of
reporting in western Massachusetts was a renewed interest in farming
among young people. The following, first of a three-part series about
a younger generation from farm families returning to their roots, visits
a century-old orchard just over the Greenfield town line in Deerfield,
where love truly seems to grow on trees.*

———

Ben Clark once loved climbing onto the boughs of the large,
spreading trees and in the treehouse his father had built for him in one
of them.

At two, Clark with his sister, Betsey, watched their father clearing
ten acres of an overgrown pasture to put in a peach orchard, dangling
their legs from the tail of a pickup while eating hot dogs grilled on the
brush piles.

These pleasures, says the thirty-two-year-old junior partner of
Clarkdale Fruit Farms, were among his favorite memories of growing
up on the Deerfield farm.

But he didn't think he'd want to come back to the farm after attending Wesleyan College any more than his father, Tom, had wanted to return after he'd left for Syracuse University. The family tradition had even deeper roots, with Tom's father, Fred, rejecting a farming life as well.

Fred, who'd left to become a coal salesman in Shelburne, returned in 1946 to the orchard his father, a physician named Webster Clark, had started in 1915 only after Webster announced he was retiring. He offered first-refusal rights to his son before selling it to a stranger. Fred took him up on the offer.

Ben had lent a hand to his grandfather Fred, loading up apples for the Greenfield Farmers' Market and then helping him sell there. The boy wasn't allowed to handle anything greater than a five-dollar bill. He was even less inclined to go into farming than his elders.

"I was a day student at Deerfield Academy with kids from places like Greenwich, Connecticut and New York," remembers Clark. "I was jealous. Now, farming and growing your own food is an 'in' thing. At the time, it was quaint. I wanted to go off and see other things."

Encouraged by parents, Tom and Becky—both of whom have fine arts degrees from Syracuse University—Ben Clark headed off to Wesleyan, much more interested in architecture than in farming.

Together with his older sister, he'd started working on the farm breaking up cartons at age eight or nine, and then picking apples at twelve or thirteen, but chores like shoveling didn't appeal to him. And any enthusiasm he may have had was dampened after hearing his parents talk about the threats of hail, frost, and drought seemingly year after year.

Clark still returned to work on the farm during the summer just as he'd been doing through adolescence, and friends who came up to visit the farm "said it was cool." But he liked the freer environment at Wesleyan and liked living on his own. And he became more involved in theater lighting and backstage work, which he did after graduation for five years in Boston and Providence.

He was living in Providence and returned to the farm briefly after his grandfather's 2005 death, which reemphasized the story of how his grandfather and then father had both returned to the farm after rejecting it and wandering off.

"I was rethinking my life plan," he recalls. "After college, people I met would ask, 'When are you going back?' There was no pressure from my parents, but it had always been a fallback plan for me to come back to. I thought I would come back and do a year as a trial run."

It turned out to be a tough adjustment when Ben Clark returned in 2006, beginning with his ten-year Deerfield Academy reunion. Then there was the fact that he didn't have friends his age who lived in the area. And on top of that, he'd just broken up with a girlfriend.

The toughest adjustment of all was going from a theater schedule—waking up bleary-eyed at ten in the morning and sometimes working until midnight—to a daily farm routine that starts at six or so and can last well until dark.

But when he began selling at the Greenfield Farmers' Market—the same setting where his grandfather's interactions with the community had piqued his interest years earlier—Clark began making friends with farmers and vendors from his own generation.

Some of them, like Caroline Pam and Tim Wilcox of The Kitchen Garden in Sunderland, were first-generation farmers whose gravitation to agriculture seemed to represent a new wave of the "back-to-the-land" movement that had drawn Clark's father home to the orchard in the early 1970s.

"It's wonderful," says the sixty-two-year-old Tom Clark of his son's return to the 104-year-old operation. "For me and for him, the good thing is going away and getting a different perspective on stuff. It's hard for anybody who's coming into a second- or third-generation business to come in with expectations that you're going to take over. I think that can be an albatross around your neck—the expectation that here's the business your grandpa made and you're going to keep it going whether you like it or not."

Tom Clark, part of Community Involved in Sustaining Agriculture when it first started up nearly thirty years ago, says that organization played an enormous role in revitalizing farming to the point where there's an appeal for young people to keep the land in production.

"Now agriculture is big, and Ben has friends his age with a similar perspective," says the elder Clark, who's also found a new connection by working side by side with his son. "It could be pretty lonely if you're the only guy who's thirty in a room full of seventy-year-old farmers."

Another recipe for success is that Lori Holmes, a Tisch School of the Arts-trained dancer and choreographer whom Ben had met during a theater production back in Providence, joined him as his wife in December 2009 to become part of the farm family and raise their sons at Clarkdale.

Just as Tom Clark began expanding what had been Fred Clark's McIntosh and Macoun apple varieties and shifted marketing away from wholesale to retail, his son found he's been able to make his own mark on the business as a co-manager transitioning to part owner.

Ben Clark has helped build the farm's website as well as set up a Facebook page and introduce credit-card sales. The website has received heavy traffic during autumn weekends, he says, and was probably responsible for a sharp reduction in the number of people phoning for directions to the orchard.

The Clarks continue diversifying, with about ten acres planted in peaches and an increasing crop of plums, grapes, cherries. They've also introduced heritage varieties of apples and pears so that the farm could introduce two new kinds of cider.

"One of the things that's really solidified me being here is that I know I'm carrying on a tradition, farming the same land," says Ben, who's been approached by older generations of customers as "Tommy's boy." Some say they remember doing business at Clarkdale when his grandfather ran it. "It's about stewardship and hoping my children will be farming the same land."

The challenges are still there, he recognizes: a heavy frost can cost Clarkdale about thirty percent of its crop. They have added to the farm's sprinkler system and have an irrigation system to protect against drought.

But when part of the crop was once damaged by hail, Clark says, it helped to know the farm has a supportive customer base that could appreciate that the damage was just cosmetic.

"We're really lucky in what we have, that there's that awareness and appreciation," says Ben, who's settled down with wife, Lori, to raise their family on the farm, with Tom and Becky just across the road. "Right now, I wouldn't rather be anywhere else."

**David Amram**

# Woody and Me

### February 19, 2009

*I'll admit that I hadn't known much about David Amram before having the opportunity to interview him as his work was about to be premiered locally by the Pioneer Valley Symphony. But as a fan of orchestral as well as folk music and jazz, I was intrigued by Amram's career and found him a delightful, quirky, and likeable personality whose story deserved to be shared.*

———

As I was walking that ribbon of highway,
I saw above me that endless skyway:
I saw below me that golden valley:
This land was made for you and me.

The year was 1956. Ahmed Bashir, a friend of jazz greats Charlie Parker, Sonny Rollins, and Charlie Mingus, was crashing at the Lower East Side apartment rented for thirty-eight dollars a month by fellow musician David Amram.

"You wanna meet Woody?" Bashir asked one morning.

"Woody who?" asked Amram. "Woody Herman?"

"No, Woody Guthrie," Bashir answered. The two men set out walking to a little apartment a few blocks—but seemingly worlds—away.

"There was Woody Guthrie—a very small, wiry man sitting at a kitchen table," remembers Amram. "And the amazing thing was he was wearing cowboy boots, and I'd never seen anyone in New York City wearing cowboy boots. And since I was brought up in a farming community of two hundred, a place called Feasterville, Pennsylvania, I could hear something familiar in his speech. The way he spoke and his accent reminded me of the farmers who used to get together at the neighborhood gas station where I grew up."

Amram recalls that the three men "sat swapping tales and drinking coffee at the tiny kitchen table from noon until it was dark outside. We sat transfixed as he took us on his journeys with him through his stories. Woody didn't need a guitar to put you under his spell, and you could tell that when he was talking to us, it wasn't an act or a routine. Like his songs and books and artwork, everything came from the heart."

Amram and Guthrie—who was already suffering from his fatal Huntington's disease but was "still so positive and full of energy"—had more in common than either man probably knew. Both were cultural sponges. Collecting an array of sounds and traditions in their open-ended "hard travelin'," everywhere they wound up, they both spread a freewill offering from what they'd gathered.

Amram—who'd moved at twelve to a "checkerboard (black-and-white) neighborhood" in Washington, DC, and learned to play piano, percussion, and French horn—had already befriended Parker and Mingus, played in California's Carmel Bach Festival, and served in the army in Korea before moving to New York.

After all that, as a part of a stew that included studying at the Manhattan School of Music as well as playing French horn with Mingus and bassist Oscar Pettiford, Amram turned his musical ear to Guthrie.

"And in this real Oklahoma drawl he was talking about all the things he was interested in knowing about," recalls Amram, a composer as well as a jazz, classical, and folk performer. "He talked about sports, about the Brooklyn Dodgers. And he talked about what it was like to go out to sea and how that gave him a chance to think about everything that happened on land and sort it out.

"And he knew that I was a jazz player and a budding composer of music," Amram continues, "and he talked about the different jazz players that he had heard and admired and about ballet and opera and classical music that he enjoyed. He was just one of those people who just had seemingly endless knowledge about so many different things."

Guthrie was an itinerant balladeer who roamed a nation struggling through the Great Depression with ears wide open to the sounds of the people. He captured and conveyed their spirit in "This Land is Your Land," the people's anthem he penned in 1940 as his antidote to Irving Berlin's "God Bless America."

In the program notes to Amram's "Symphonic Variations on a Song by Woody Guthrie," premiered by Pioneer Valley Symphony at Northampton's Academy of Music, Amram writes, "When Woody wrote his classic song, 'This Land is Your Land,' the ideals he expressed were not rhetoric or New Age hot air. Times were tough, but he saw he had a job to do to make things better. As we enter hard times today, his philosophy as well as his art ring true, and make us all feel more connected."

> When the sun came shining, and I was strolling,
> And the wheat fields waving and the dust clouds rolling,
> As the fog was lifting a voice was chanting:
> This land was made for you and me.

Like Guthrie, David Amram is a boundless, wide-eyed pied piper defying easy categorization.

He's collaborated with Leonard Bernstein, Jack Kerouac, Steve Martin, Langston Hughes, Dizzy Gillespie, Dustin Hoffman, Thelonious Monk, Odetta, Elia Kazan, Arthur Miller, Lionel Hampton, E. G. Marshall, Tito Puente, and Willie Nelson.

Amram has composed more than a hundred orchestral and chamber music works, scores for theater and film—including *The Manchurian Candidate* and *Splendor in The Grass,* and two operas, including the ground-breaking Holocaust opera *The Final Ingredient.*

The most recent of his three books is *Upbeat: Nine Lives of a Musical Cat.*

A flute concerto, "Giants in the Night," commissioned by Sir James Galway, is dedicated to the memory of Parker, Kerouac, and Gillespie. With author Frank McCourt, Amram also created an original setting of the Mass, "*Missa Manhattan.*"

And, on the night before he came to the Pioneer Valley for a public lecture and demonstration at Stoneleigh-Burnham School in Greenfield and the concert in Northampton, Amram took part along with Harry Belafonte, Pete Seeger, and others in a memorial tribute to folk legend Odetta at Manhattan's Riverside Church.

> In the squares of the city, in the shadow of the steeple,
> By the relief office I seen my people;
> As they stood there hungry, I stood there asking
> Is this land made for you and me?

A crowd of thousands sang along when Seeger, 89, and Bruce Springsteen led a rousing finale to the Obama inaugural concert in front of the Lincoln Memorial.

Amram was commissioned by Guthrie's daughter Nora to compose "symphonic variations" on the anthem. The Silicon Valley Symphony premiered the variations. In Amram's work, the timeless melody travels, as Woody did, from an Oklahoma stomp dance and an Okemah, Oklahoma church service to a Pampa, Texas, barn dance with a stopover in Mexico and a Dustbowl dirge. Then, it lands in New York's ethnic neighborhoods with a Caribbean street festival, a klezmer-accented Jewish wedding, a Middle Eastern bazaar, and a Salvation Army hymn.

"All this influenced him in that beautiful song that he wrote," says Amram. "Nora told me Woody loved to walk through those places and had an enormous interest in the foods, cultures, music and languages. People like Woody, Pete Seeger, and the great Odetta were doing what they call ethnomusicology before that existed."

Amram, 78, who plays twenty-five musical folk instruments from around the world including piano and jazz French horn, is no slouch himself when it comes to mixing it up and getting down.

"My approach is not to be a great Burger King of music—fast-food franchiser—and put everything into one brand but rather to celebrate all these precious, beautiful things I just bumped into in my travels and was receptive to."

Amram likens his approach to what other composers before him have done: he writes what he knows and feels in his heart. "When I started doing this as a teenager back in the 'forties, any kind of career counselor would have said I either had a multiple-personality disorder, was schizophrenic, or had a career death wish."

In a 1960s magazine interview, Amram claimed that his greatest musical influences were Bach, Mozart, Gillespie, Monk, and countless country, Cajun, and Middle Eastern musicians. A response came from the management of the New York Philharmonic—where Amram had just been named the orchestra's first-ever composer in residence: "How can you equate barroom entertainers with the treasures of European music?"

Amram's answer: "It's the purity of intent and an exquisite choice of notes. That's what determines it all."

Amram appeared as composer-in-residence at the 2008 Democratic National Convention where he conducted his 1969 "Three Songs for America," a setting of words by John F. Kennedy, Martin Luther King, and Robert F. Kennedy. He also performed Parker's "Now's the Time" and led the Colorado Children's Chorus in a composition based on Native American themes he'd learned a half-century ago.

"I always try to pay attention," Amram says. "If I can really do it correctly—in terms of phrasing, nuance, rhythm, and style—then when I actually play it front of people, I'm not putting on a costume and misrepresenting something, but sharing something that I've been blessed to learn."

> I've roamed and rambled and I followed my footsteps
> To the sparkling sands of her diamond deserts;
> And all around me a voice was sounding:
> This land was made for you and me.

Nora Guthrie sent Amram off to the annual WoodyFest in Okemah, Woody's birthplace, to get a clearer sense of the roots of the iconic song and the man who wrote it. Amram jammed with musicians there and met with fans, friends, and family, including Guthrie's sister.

She'd grown up with Aaron Copland's *"Appalachian Spring"* because her mother, Marjorie Guthrie, was in the original Martha Graham ballet production and always thought of her father's song as carrying on the tradition of the "Simple Gifts" Shaker melody incorporated into Copland's score.

Rather than suggesting he concoct just another "pop-shlock" arrangement of her father's iconic song, she asked Amram to express some of its truer meanings.

He imagined Guthrie hearing the melody first as a church hymn that he then carried in his head as he traveled from place to place.

Amram pointed to Kerouac—with whom he collaborated in the first-ever jazz poetry reading in New York in 1957 and then in the years that followed—as another inspirational, innovating pioneer like Guthrie.

"Kerouac celebrated the commonplace, beautiful, everyday things in American life that a lot of intellectuals thought were not worthy of consideration," recalls Amram. "He, Woody, and all the great artists of history really knew how to pay attention to everything and never to disrespect any person or any situation because everything has something to offer."

Nobody living can ever stop me,
As I go walking that freedom highway;
Nobody living can ever make me turn back
This land was made for you and me

In his travels, says Amram, Guthrie managed "to look around and celebrate and rejoice in what's here and share those blessings. Wherever he went, he was open and receptive. He welcomed and found out a lot of things most people just ignored."

At the beginning of Obama's presidency, given the hard times, the public outcry for leadership and the harkening back to the FDR and Lincoln eras, Amram saw a timeliness in re-presenting Guthrie's strong, hopeful tone, "trying to celebrate the continuity and the harmony we have, despite our many differences. The way it resonates in these particular times is almost biblical."

With his Guthrie-inspired work heard in the Pioneer Valley, Amram reflects, "I hope it pulses with the rhythms of our challenges and that we feel like dancing through them! I hope we feel our own much-needed strength in it. I hope it touches our national soul."

Curt Culver plowing in the documentary *Root Hog or Die*

# *Root Hog or Die*

## August 18, 2012

*Franklin County filmmaker Rawn Fulton's documentary,* Root Hog or Die, *made shortly after I arrived in western Massachusetts, is so fundamental to appreciating the traditional Yankee culture that's fading that I believe it should be required viewing. I can't begin to keep track of how many times I've watched the film, always amazed at how vividly and completely it captures the spirit of rural self-reliance.*

---

"We're a timeless people. We don't try to do things by eight-to-five," says the voice of farmer Charlie Culver of Ashfield, as his son drives a team of workhorses, plowing uphill for what seems like forever.

"We do it as we go along. We pay no attention to the time, the clock. We just do what's got to be done when it's got to be done. And our work's not that objectionable to us. We don't ever stop."

To say there's a timeless quality to the images and the voices, in Rawn Fulton's black-and-white, hour-long documentary *Root Hog or Die* is to belabor the obvious. Yet so much has changed in Franklin

County over the forty-eight years since the Bernardston filmmaker first made the film that it's worth viewing with fresh eyes. Especially since there's a keen reawakening of interest in protecting what remains of farming and rural values today.

Locavores, sustainability, and green living would have been foreign words to old-timers like Herman Severance of Greenfield and Herman Streeter of Bernardston—two of the many farmers around Franklin County and neighboring Windham County, Vermont interviewed by Fulton in 1975. That was soon after Fulton arrived with his wife from Brooklyn after growing up in a southern Connecticut town that had been comparable twenty years earlier in size and life rhythms to Bernardston.

The idea for a film about the Yankee farming lifestyle came, ironically, from a developer named David Berelson, who'd built Bernardston's Crumpin-Fox Golf Course and hilltop restaurant The Phases. He kept running into—and uprooting—farmers who seemed to be living much as their ancestors had.

"How'd you like to make a film about the farmers around here?" Berelson, son of noted University of Chicago behavioral scientist Bernard Berelson, asked Fulton when he first met him at a cookout and learned he was a filmmaker.

Fulton was twenty-six. Together with his wife during their two years in the Peace Corps, he had already made the twenty-five-minute film "Sun River" about working with India's Adivasi indigenous people.

Arriving in Bernardston in 1972, Fulton found a town that had as many people as his hometown, Newtown, Connecticut, had in 1952.

"There were still the farmers, still the dairies, still the connection to that way of life that I'd grown up with and really loved being around. Berelson could feel and taste the uniqueness of it, so he was very excited about capturing it on film before it all disappeared."

Fulton—who looks more than a bit like actor Jeff Bridges—had been roommates with Knowlton "Terry" Noyes for three years at Columbia University. Noyes had been living on a Virginia farm when Fulton approached him about joining him on the project. Fulton turned to Bernardston auctioneer Louis Pratt for ideas about the best people to include in the portrait of "an agrarian, dairy lifestyle."

The focus was on the kind of small, traditional hill farms that had dotted towns like Ashfield, Colrain, and Leyden for generations—not the "giant, industrialized, flatland Connecticut-River farms" in the valley.

"We were interested in capturing a sense of what these people were like and what they had to say," says Fulton, whose Searchlight Films—based in his home overlooking Butch Grover's Bernardston hayfields—has more than thirty-five documentary productions to its credit.

But Pratt and others warned that those Yankee farmers weren't apt to say much, especially to a couple of young urban types pointing camera equipment and microphones at them.

"They said, 'These people are very laconic. They're going to say two words and walk off and do their chores. And one of them will be 'A-yup,' and one of them will be, 'Nope.'"

Without even calling ahead, Fulton and Noyes drove to see the farmers on Pratt's list. It was 1973.

"I realized after the first two or three that the worst thing I could do was to leave the camera in the car," recalls Fulton, "because they would inevitably say something fantastic they'd never say again, at least not in the same way. So after the first three or four encounters, we just learned to get out with the camera rolling and say, 'Hi.'"

The result of a year or so of such visits is a portrait of rural Americana as dramatic and evocative as anything by painters Thomas Hart Benton or Grant Wood. But the black-and-white depiction of agrarian Franklin County, circa 1975, is punctuated by the sounds of down-to-earth Yankees describing, just as plain as horse droppings and ax chopping, the day-in, day-out realities of hardscrabble life in and around the region.

"Far from being laconic, once the people we met realized we were seriously interested in listening, we couldn't stop them," remembers Fulton. "It's like you opened a valve and this stuff kept pouring out, like they'd been waiting their whole lives to tell somebody."

"Before I was twenty-one," a white-haired Linwood Lesure of Ashfield's Watson section tells the camera, "I went to an auction with $175 I had saved up and they sold a farm of about 140 acres with a house and barn. It sold for $3,850 and I got it. I borrowed the money and paid for the farm."

Minnie Richardson of Leyden, nearly eighty, says, "That's one thing: you can't starve on a farm if you've got any guts at all. In the summertime, we'd itemize the things on the table in front of us that we'd have to purchase from the store."

And Fred Call, after filling a yacht-sized sedan with 41.9-cent gasoline at Call's Garage in Colrain back then in 1973, tells a customer how a nickel change isn't still enough to buy a candy bar, which is smaller than it used to be and double the price. "I don't know where it's gonna end," he says. Then he recalls old-timer Newton Carpenter telling him about forty active farms lining the road where only three remained "and now none are being used. There's just summer people."

The film, shot using available light in sixteen-millimeter reversal to maximize image quality, has long, extended shots of tending open landscape that convey the unhurried lifestyle and laborious days of tilling, plowing, harvesting, logging, and sugaring. Its title, *Root Hog or Die*, derives from a pre-Civil War saying denoting independence and comes from a line spoken by Louis Black of Leyden near the film's opening, which shows a still image of an old horse-drawn plow.

"We raised our own pork, beef, potatoes," he says in a close-up of his weathered face. "There was no welfare business then. It was either root, hog, or die. You had to work for a living. You couldn't ask the town for any help. You wouldn't get it."

As a young filmmaker who'd cut his teeth on documenting communal life in rural India, Fulton says he wanted the conversations about family, community, work, and neighborliness to reflect an entire way of life that almost seems rooted in the rocky soil.

From Francis Barnard in Shelburne and Stevens Dole in Shelburne to Louise Taylor in Bernardston and Fred Lincoln in Warwick, "Each of them had their own special personality and style and accent and perspective," remembers Fulton, who intentionally sought out those farmers who'd never stopped using horse-drawn equipment. "We thought it would be more authentic looking or more traditional.

"We wanted things to be absolutely as natural, as uncomposed as possible. We also shot it in black and white because we wanted it to feel old even when it was new. Now that it's more than forty years old, it really is old."

Fulton calls the finished film "a portrait of a way of life as presented by people who were toward the end of their own lives, but was also toward the end of the entire movement."

Although they had survived in some cases for generations, those family businesses—dependent on everyone pitching in for long days of hard labor that they not only took in stride but savored as part of the rhythm of life—were strained and gave way as rising costs and competing economic realities became unbearable. Gradually, many were forced to seek work off their small farms just to make ends meet, "but they always kept chickens, a couple hogs, four or five cows as part of their whole sense of what's real."

Sid Gaines of Guilford, Vermont, recalls, "In 1910, even with town taxes and all, I could get by on two or three hundred dollars a year. I could go to the next-door neighbor and say, 'Can you help me tomorrow?' and I'd be sure he'd be here without money changing hands."

But one farm with more than a hundred cows now exists where eight families once lived with maybe fourteen cows. Otherwise, the land has given way to people who have a house and commute to work in town.

"Now the folks just live there, and they don't got no use for the land," Gaines concludes.

In one memorable moment of the film, Dole tells about how his grandfather built his house and barn in 1858 and 1859, waking up at 2:30 AM each morning to drive his two yoked oxen 15 miles from Shelburne to Guilford and back to haul the slate needed for roofs.

## Archetypal Moments

The only music in the film, other than the unaccompanied farmer's singing that opens and closes it, comes from the fiddle music at a late summer square dance at Bernardston's Kiwanis Park.

Fulton's camera pulls back into night darkness, dancers still visible in the distance, and the scene dissolves into one of a field of harvested corn in Ashfield, set against the hills in the background, then focusing on a single milkweed pod with the lone remaining sound a rush of wind as only the shadows of clouds move across the field.

"There was a lot of people in these hills," says the deep, folksy voice of Norman Field of Bernardston. "They all had pretty small farms. No big acreage. If you go up along the ridge, along the state

21

line, you'll find cellar holes and stone walls, and now it's all woods. New England was pretty crowded before the Civil War. After the Civil War, they opened up the West. You could go and get a farm in 'Ioway' just for moving onto it. A lot of people here moved out there.

"Too small.

"Too hilly.

"Stony.

"Didn't pay."

Fulton, who imitates the slow, measured pacing of Field's voice with proud mastery, reflects back on that sequence.

"There are some moments in this film that are archetypal. I can't believe we did it.

"When we started out, we didn't have a script. We had a list of names on a piece of paper, and go see what you find out. And we started filming in the spring, in sugaring time. We filmed all summer into fall and early winter. And the film is cut in that sequence. It was like this is what they did, this is how they said it, this is what came out following the form of the year, following the time of the agrarian progression. It was unintentional, and it was perfect because this is the way these people's lives are organized."

### Pachelbel

Just as *Root Hog* tells the story of the people, there's a story as well behind the film, of course.

Berelson, who first conceived of the documentary, agreed to fund the filming, which was done on the cheap. But when the Arab oil embargo of 1973 hit and his own finances began to tighten, he told Fulton and Noyes that he'd simply run out of money for editing to continue.

For about five years, Fulton recalls, *Root Hog* simply sat on the shelf until Noyes—whose family had published the *Washington Evening Star* and helped found the Associated Press—thought of applying for National Endowment for the Arts funding to complete the project.

Berelson approached the National Fund for the Arts as well as WGBY, the public television station in Springfield, and Greenfield Community College Foundation for funding, and, eventually, Berelson handed over ownership of the film to the foundation.

The peaceful spirit of nature that pervades the hour-long documentary was almost broken when Fulton and his financier came to loggerheads. Berelson, perhaps influenced by the wild popularity of the mesmerizing Pachelbel's "Canon"—used later throughout the Hollywood movie Ordinary People—insisted that the seventeenth-century music run during the end credits for *Root Hog or Die*.

"I said, 'I don't think so,'" recalls Fulton. "This film has no music in it at all except for the square dance. It's all cinema verité, it's all very spare, it's all understated, all immersion. We're not going to stick in Beethoven or Albinoni or Pachelbel at the last minute and change everything."

Berelson was so upset by the refusal of Fulton, Noyes and WGBY's Dan Kain—who had taken on the role of the film's executive producer—that he stormed out of the project and his friendship with Futon. "He basically never spoke to me again," Fulton remembers.

Berelson died in 1988.

The documentary was shown on public television and won prizes at the New England, Chicago, and Houston film festivals and bronze awards at the New York and American film festivals as well as a New England Emmy Award.

Although it's among the earliest films in a list that includes works on world population and the environment, Pre-Colombian and Native American cultures, portraits of artists and authors Ezra Jack Keats and Virginia Lee Burton and more, Fulton takes pride in *Root Hog or Die* as one of his best feature-length films.

"I think it belongs in every American studies program in the US and Canada and around the world. This is Americana at its absolute most basic and best," he says. "What makes this film timely is the same thing that makes it timeless. There are deeper forces at work here by myopically putting on blinders and going to work every day, every day, every day. In what we do, we miss the connection between the now and the infinite. We miss the big picture. What makes this film special is that you have a localized portrait of the local situation and yet it does it in a way that's global."

Fulton believes there seems to be a reawakening—just as there was in the 1960s—of some of the values expressed in the film by people like Isabel Slate of Bernardston: "I'm next to the soil, and you see all these things, and you certainly can't help but believe there's a God."

"All the things in the sixties and seventies, we thought our generation was discovering she and her neighbors had grown up with and were already part of her DNA," Fulton says. "And this is what I think is the value of the film, what makes it timeless. We're now rediscovering things that they already knew. That's the full circle aspect of it. The film has kind of a permanent sense of connection to long-range values, long-range goals, long-range principles of organizing not just what we do but how we see and how we feel."

In the film, Charlie Culver of Ashfield recalls the "gruesome" Depression of the 1930s but how some relatives who had "lorded it over us" after they had moved to the city returned home to the farm rather than having to stand three to five hours in a line to get a loaf of bread.

"They had come down to our level," Culver declares. "That's what we need right now. There's got to come a day of reckoning sometime. We can't live artificially forever."

If, as Fulton believes, there's renewed energy to relearn basic skills for living off the land and to regain some of the resilience that those old-timers have, what seems even more important is the return to their sense of values.

There's a gentle balance in *Root Hog* that reflects the simple, yet rugged, approach to life in the backwoods of Franklin County four decades ago.

"Oh, it's a good miss," Norman Fields says after a farm auction scene in the documentary. "You do miss 'em once in a while. There's a little pride of ownership and so forth, of being in business for yourself and having plenty of cows. But seven days a week: that ain't worth it."

Fields's emotional words are followed immediately by those of Louise Taylor as she feeds her calves on her Bernardston farm.

"Maybe it's a hard way of life. But in some ways, it's quite gratifying," she offers quietly. "When we came here, we came on what you'd call a shoestring, and it has been a struggle ever since we've been here. I think some people don't get any thrill out of having to pull hard to make both ends meet. But I find it fascinating.

"Good thing I do."

**Blanche Moyse**

# Blanche, the Bach Dynamo

### October 16, 1997

*I first heard about the living legend Blanche Moyse from a newsroom assistant who used to sing in the Blanche Moyse Chorale. Her stories along with my own love of Bach inspired me to visit the nearby Vermont community of Marlboro to investigate. I was instantly captivated by Blanche's gentle, passionate charisma as well as the music she inspired.*

----

Johann Sebastian Bach's *Magnificat* is monumental in its glory and grandeur.

So is Blanche Honnegger Moyse's reputation as a musician and choral director.

With as many years to her credit as a grand piano has keys, the silver-haired dynamo breathes magnificence into the New England Bach Festival as its founding artistic director.

The twenty-ninth annual festival, which will conclude Sunday afternoon with a performance by pianist Peter Serkin, combines the glory that is Bach with the splendor of an autumnal southern Vermont setting.

Members of the thirty-five-voice Blanche Moyse Chorale, which will perform Bach's *Magnificat* as part of the festival's opening concert at Marlboro College, are as devoted to their indefatigable Swiss-born director as she is to the music itself.

"I would die for her," says Peter Snedecor, who is in his fourth year singing bass with the chorale after singing with choirs in Cleveland and Philadelphia. "She's easily the finest conductor I've ever sung with. This is the best music I've ever had. She is a joy to sing for."

Moyse, at eighty-eight, demands the best from her singers at twice-weekly, year-round rehearsals where her passion for perfection is legendary.

"Her expectation is that you'll come to rehearsal every night to perform as a soloist might," Snedecor says. "She expects us to learn the notes on our own and to know the music very well."

In the last weeks of preparation for the upcoming festival, "We've had eleven rehearsals over fourteen nights. And she will work even harder."

In a state where seemingly every car bumper shouts out Bernie in support of the Green Mountain state's singular congressman, Moyse, too, is a Vermont folk hero and also the subject of an hour-long video documentary, *Blanche*.

Soprano Beth-Ann Betz says, "She's incredibly astute and on the ball . . . very, very nurturing in a spiritual way as well as musical. It's the experience of a lifetime."

To watch the silver-topped wonder wring glory from every measure of the score that is before her, actually kneading the chorale and instruments with one outstretched hand, then the other, is to know that Blanche Moyse is consumed with the music she has so internalized. She is bathed in Bach, and the intensity of each singer, every instrumentalist, bubbles up from her own verve.

Moyse, who came to Marlboro College in its infancy to found its music department and chair it from 1949 to 1989, has the score of each cantata and masterwork committed to memory.

"This obliges you to get so much detail in your head that you're much more aware of everything inside," she says in an accent that echoes the flourishes of her native French tongue. "It's like you have a better microscope every time."

Yet despite the countless times she's heard and performed Bach's works since her youth in Geneva, Moyse says, "Each time it's new. Each time I wonder how I could ignore so much of it the last time and be so amazed at how rich it is. Even if I do the *St. Matthew Passion*, which I did several years ago in New York, I would again find something new."

Beginning with piano lessons at age three and violin at age five, the youngest of five children was hand-picked at twelve by noted violinist Adolf Bush to leave her only formal schooling in non-musical subjects to study professionally with him.

"I have five doctorates, and each time I'm given one, I have to laugh that people don't know they're giving a doctorate to an illiterate person," jokes Moyse, who was home-tutored by her grandmother and others.

A first-prize winner in violin from the Geneva Conservatory of Music, Moyse also studied with violinist Georges Enesco, guitarist Andres Segovia, and harpsichordist Wanda Landowska. She toured throughout Europe from 1933 to 1947 as a soloist with her husband, pianist Louis Moyse, and father-in-law, Marcel Moyse, before the entire Moyse Trio was invited to Marlboro by Bush and his son-in-law, pianist Rudolf Serkin, who had been refugees from Nazi Germany. Serkin was the father of pianist Peter Serkin.

When she arrived on November 14, 1949 to teach the experimental college's small enrollment of mostly recent veterans, Moyse remembers, they seemed unfamiliar with classical music. One month later, she led them in a performance of a Bach cantata.

Moyse also founded the Brattleboro Music Center in 1952 and led a community chorus that performed at the Bach festival until she created her select chorus about forty-five years ago. The chorale performs at the two-week festival each year as well as one cantata concert as part of the summertime Marlboro Music Festival and often one or two other concerts during the year, in Vermont and occasionally on tour.

Trained as a violinist rather than a singer, Moyse nevertheless says, "I work with singers easier than with anyone else because singers have so much to do with their feelings. It's clear to them what the feelings are because you have the words."

Instead of delving into technique, "I talk about quality of the sound, in relation to feeling. If people have chosen to work with me, then I can be demanding. It's not for fun, it's for something beautiful, so it deserves to meet my demands."

Chorale members like Elizabeth "Betsy" Peck, are more than willing to oblige.

"I feel lucky to be one of her musical tools," says the soprano, who has sung with the chorale for five years. "She wants to work on the inner qualities of the music."

Serena Smith, an alto who is president of the chorale, says, "I'm very much in awe of her. She's indomitable. She's second to none."

Moyse uses an uncanny, sometimes stinging wit, delivered with her French accent, to cut through her intense rehearsals.

"If you are as annoyed with me as I am with you," she told the singers once, "you must be really pissed."

She'll turn to the altos and describe the extended note she expects from them as "a long noodle" or reproach the basses for singing too forcefully: "You know that basses don't eat little children. You sound ferocious!"

Moyse rehearses without accompaniment because "that forces people to be so much better, so much more accurate. They can't hide against anything. And there, nobody can escape me."

But recognizing that some singers were not up to the pressure, she reflects, "I've had to learn how to criticize people without offending or making them desperate. I was offending people left and right, all the time."

Sitting against a crocheted afghan in Guilford Community Church, Moyse taps out a single note on the portable Casio keyboard lying just beyond the score on a hand-built podium desk. The sopranos—whom she's asked once again to sing in unison rather than as soloists sharing the same part—have gotten out of tune, and she is bringing them back.

"I have a hearing aid, but I still hear music quite well," the maestro will say afterward. "When they are singing softly, I think it is just ideal. I can hear soft and beautiful, and I usually take my hearing aid off because I hear more faithfully the quality of the tone."

This evening's rehearsal will go until 10 or 10:30. But "I don't find that tiring at all. I'm sitting all the time. I never notice that we should take a break. I have to say, 'Please tell me when it's time to take a break.'"

Although three weeks of back-to-back rehearsals will leave her feeling a bit worn after the festival, Moyse relaxes religiously with a morning bath . . . and with the music that she recalls brought her to tears as she once sang walking through fields in Switzerland.

"If you do something you love, you don't get tired. It is much less tiring to do than my housework.

In fact, she confides, "I am ageless."

Moyse hopes to lead her chorale in a third New York performance when she turns ninety. She recalls the glory of the Carnegie Hall concert they did a few years ago and knowing that the standing ovation from the audience came not because they love her—as she knows her Vermonters do—but because they were captivated by the music, as she was.

Other than that vision, she says, "I don't think of the future. I live from day to day.

"The thing I know I would like is to work to my last day, and to have a heart attack right there. That would be ideal. I always tell my children and friends if I die on stage, don't think it's a catastrophe. It's the best gift I can receive. I hope I don't have to stop before I die."

And yet Moyse did have to stop performing the violin, which she recalls playing even as she simultaneously directed the chorale for many years. Even the first New York performance fifty years ago was done without a conductor. After twenty years of doctor visits here and in Europe, an arthritis-like pain stopped her from playing when she reached her late fifties, she recalls sadly.

"I pretend not to be a conductor," Moyse says. "I am a frustrated violinist. What I really loved was when I could still be playing with my normal skills and I could be the first chair of the orchestra. I don't like very much to be called a conductor; I'm a musician. My musicians know very well I'm one of them."

*Blanche Moyse, awarded the Alfred Nash Patterson Lifetime Achievement Award by Choral Arts New England in 2000, died at her Brattleboro home in 2011 at 101.*

a scene from *The Cummington Story*

# *The Cummington Story*

## April 30, 2005

*The following is an example of how one story often begets another. Cummington, the Hampshire County town I initially passed through heading across the Berkshires to Franklin County for my first visit to what would someday become home, has always held fascination for me. The film, which I'd heard of because of its Aaron Copland connection, was mentioned by a former town resident I was interviewing on the opposite end of the county for a series on high-tech cottage industries. As always, I made a note of the possible story to pursue as soon as I could.* ____

The town meeting is like almost any other with a stern-looking moderator looking out over a town hall packed with intent-looking residents.

But this particular meeting, captured on black-and-white film, is a seventy-five-year-old propaganda piece that tells *The Cummington Story*, a fictionalized account of a resettlement project that helped nearly fifty World War II refugees find their way to new lives.

Back then, fourteen-year-old Gloria Gowdy was a neighbor who helped the German and Austrian newcomers learn English.

William Streeter was a thirteen-year-old boy who was asked to appear as an extra in the church scene of the film, released seventy-five years ago to show the world how a typical New England village welcomed European refugees.

"When the refugees came, the kids lumped them all together as foreigners, not to be trusted," he recalls now. "We'd follow them. One night, a group of them came in on a Greyhound bus, and after they went to the pastor's red house, I found some American Express checks rolled up. I knocked on the door, and they broke into tears, they were so happy to get that."

Stephen Howes, who was six in 1945, was warned to stay away from the strangers.

"There was suspicion about who they were, why they were here, what kids they were going to snap up," says Howes, now Cummington Historical Society chairman.

Several of those refugees, who appear in the film with fictionalized names, had been noted artists, craftspeople, and literary figures beginning life anew. Some settled at least briefly in Northfield, although most moved on. The refugees—most of them Jews—navigated an uneasy relationship with the Yankee townsfolk in a time rife with wartime tensions.

From its Norman Rockwell-like images of town meeting, church, farms, and village scenes, the twenty-minute film produced by the US Overseas War Information Bureau captures a slice of a simpler time here when even Route 9 passing directly through this Hampshire County village wasn't enough to disturb its quiet. The highway now bypasses Main Street.

What did shake Cummington, just a stone's throw from Ashfield and Plainfield, was the initiative of its Congregationalist minister to take action as the war loomed. The Reverend Carl Sangree, a conscientious objector during World War I, asked Douglas Horton of the General Council of Congregational Christian Churches what a minister could do other than support the war. Told to "take care of the refugees," Sangree was appalled at Horton "giving me a mop and asking me to stop a flood."

More than simply offering food and a place to sleep, Sangree wanted to give refugees a way to support themselves.

Horton told Sangree, who narrates *The Cummington Story*, that the church council could provide ten thousand dollars to set up a refugee program. That money never came, but Sangree raised what contributions he could from donors including the Reverend Roland Johnson of Ashfield. The pastor also offered his own house in Cummington—the little red house—for up to a dozen refugees at a time between May 1940 and September 1944.

Beginning with Johannes Hans Gaides, a German political prisoner who had escaped two concentration camps, the refugees arrived. Most came through New York and were part of mixed Jewish-Christian couples who Sangree felt would fall through the cracks of other refugee programs.

"I could see him every day working in his garden," recalls Gowdy of Gaides, the large, university-trained agricultural economist who went on to study at Harvard University. "Everybody watched him in his garden."

As the fictionalized documentary film depicts, Sangree tried to melt some of the chill of townspeople toward the refugees, from the attitude of the "old stove league" at Ed Hall's grocery to a stiff reception by those attending a church service.

Mrs. Hall, for example, is shown scowling as she waits on the film's main character, Joseph. "And that wasn't acting!" remembers Gowdy.

## Life in Cummington

The film captures the rhythm of small-town life: schoolchildren trudging home, and townsfolk raking leaves, hanging out wash, or stacking wood.

There's a hint, though, that Cummington is a town where culture and common folk sometimes clash. It was the birthplace of poet William Cullen Bryant and home of *the Cummington Press* as well as Greenwood Music Camp and the Cummington School of the Arts. And yet some locals referred to another summer camp, Meadowbrook Lodge, as "the Jew camp," says Streeter.

"The town was interesting because it had an intellectual side and an old Yankee side to it that forced the two sides to reconcile where they were in life."

Sangree's first-person film narration describes the tension between locals and strangers, which he helped melt away by the movie's end through a kind of occupational therapy that helps both groups feel more comfortable with one another.

"I've always felt the strangeness between people breaks down when they live and work and meet together as neighbors," Sangree narrates.

Yet the 1945 film, eventually translated into more than twenty languages including Afghan, Arabic, Chinese, and Urdu, doesn't convey how much Sangree himself was viewed with suspicion.

"He was an outsider," remembers Streeter, author of the town history. "He was an intellect, and oftentimes, local people rub the wrong way with intellects."

The pastor was suspect, as much as anything, "because he played basketball on Sundays, and those were Puritan people who didn't approve of such fun on a the sabbath," recalls Howes.

When the US declared war on Japan in December 1941, Sangree wrote, a kind of hysteria erupted in town, with some villagers threatening to shoot the refugees, believing they were spies. They were confined to the hostel and brought their mail and food until the quarantine was lifted.

"The minister has difficulties with the villagers who are opposed to the presence of foreigners here and to the existence of the hostel," refugee Paul Amann related to his wife in a 1942 letter. "On Sunday, there was hardly anyone in church to listen to his sermon. A piece of paper was circulated soliciting signatures to have the minister dismissed and to look for a new pastor, one who would take a greater interest in the community than in the refugees. Sangree seems to be an independent thinker and a man of some means at that."

Amann wrote, too, that one refugee couple, the Koenisbergers "were able to buy a house and start their own business, which some of the villagers view with suspicion, alarmed that these foreigners might turn out to be competitors for local craftspeople."

With the help of spy rumors, wrote Sangree, "the Cummington hostel had a lot of free publicity and notoriety, which instead of destroying the project promoted it."

Some of those rumors boiled over, with an FBI agent showing up one morning at the hostel to investigate a report of a Bund meeting at which a Nazi had allegedly addressed a hundred Germans. As it turned out, the speaker, exiled former Frankfurt newspaper editor Hans Kallman, had been speaking to the local PTA about the democratic movement in Austria before the Nazi takeover.

"There was suspicion regarding the refugees," Gowdy recalls, "not only because they were German or Jewish but because they were outsiders . . . and many people believed they could be spies."

Gowdy, whose Jewish father, Herman Goldsmith, ran Goldy's auto garage in town and was the first to sign the hostel's guest book, recalls an incident early on:

"Some people heard a tapping coming nightly from an open upstairs window at the hostel and came to my father to wonder if someone was sending messages by wire. My father spoke to Mr. Gaides, who confessed that at night he went upstairs after a hard day's work to compose love letters on his typewriter to his lady love in England."

What won many Cummington residents over, ultimately, was seeing how hard the refugees worked, remembers Gowdy. And Sangree worked just as hard to help them find new lives.

"Cummington Hostel is really a craft house—a home where we provide all the security and friendship that an American home can provide while refugees are working in their arts and crafts," wrote the pastor. "We guide them in their work by our advice and provide materials. We try to find a market for their goods or a place for their skills."

Amann, whom Sangree had speak at West Cummington Church in 1942, wrote to his wife, "I was the main attraction with my talk about our refugee experiences. People complimented me on my good English, which was good to hear, for when picking apples, I often don't speak a word to anyone for most of the day."

He later wrote to Sangree, "Looking back on my stay at the guest-house, I fully realize what a blessing have been these months of quiet preparation for an American life."

### Making a Film

*The Cummington Story* itself was something of an accident for the little town.

Yet in part because of a musical score written over one week by noted composer Aaron Copland, it is the best known of *The American Scene* propaganda films, envisioned as a means of paving the way for

US occupation of postwar Europe by showing favorable images of Americans in the Midwest, Northwest, South, and New England.

On his way to find a setting in Maine for the last film in the fourteen-part series, screenwriter and part-time area resident Howard Southgate Smith stopped off in Cummington to visit Sangree, whom he had known from earlier days. The pastor convinced the filmmaker from neighboring Goshen to visit the refugee hostel, and Southgate decided there was no need to travel to Maine.

Cummington's agricultural fair, cultural richness, long main street with a white church, village store, and particularly its refugee hostel won the town the title role for the "re-enacted documentary" cataloged by the National Archives as the integration of a group of World War II refugees into the life of the small town of Cummington, Massachusetts. The town's clergyman describes the town's initial coolness towards the diffident newcomers and helps involve them in social, church and vocational activities. Individual refugees find familiar work in printing, farming, lumbering and shop keeping and begin socializing with their neighbors, as a "new kind of respect" develops on both sides, includes panoramic views of the countryside in and around the town.

The Museum of Modern Art describes *The Cummington Story* "as unaffected and moving a sermon against insularity and intolerance as could well be imagined." As a propaganda film, it never mentions that some of the refugees are Jewish nor where they come from nor the persecution they suffered.

In the final days of the hostel's operation in the fall of 1944, swarms of film-crew members rolled into Cummington for three months, complete with a seventeen-ton electric generator truck to provide thirty kilowatts of power.

Called in with other townspeople at the last minute to help fill up the pews for the "stern-faced" church scene, Streeter recalls the "carnival" atmosphere when the production crew came to the tiny town.

"It was like Hollywood with big trucks, big generators, everyone peeking to see what was going on," he remembers. To this day, "They're so damned proud of it, you can't imagine."

Using government station wagons, the crew shot actual footage at the Cummington Fair, horse-race scenes in Great Barrington, and exterior and interior church scenes at the West Cummington and Cummington Village churches, respectively.

"The people in the church scene," says Gowdy, "probably half of them had never seen the inside of that church. The people were given a church supper for hanging around all day."

Virginia Caldwell, who lived next door to the red house recalls that her father, Leon Stevens, was shown in the town-meeting scene standing up to speak. The scene was shot over two days, and he was sent home on the second day to wear the same tie he'd worn on the first.

"It was a big deal," remembers Caldwell, who was eighteen at the time. "Here was a small town in a film that's been translated into a number of languages."

The film, shown at Tanglewood Music Center in 2000 as part of a centennial tribute to Copland, is presented in Cummington each summer but is rarely seen elsewhere.

"What would be better than to make a documentary about Germans and Austrians who were forced out, to show the richness of American culture, its tradition of civil responsibility and democracy, to show how people coming from their own lands could be assimilated into the culture, how they learned to negotiate its values into their own background?" asks Smith College Professor Gertraud Gutzmann, who emigrated from Germany to learn English in Pittsfield in 1960.

"The irony was that it shows Koenigsberger returning to Austria, bringing home democratic values. He never returned to the US."

## Changing Attitudes

Sangree, who served as minister in Cummington until 1946, didn't end his peace work with Cummington.

After the death of his wife, he and his second wife, former Northfield School Assistant President Florence Lyon, met with André Trocme, whose French village's rescue of thousands of Jews from the Nazis was later portrayed in the book, Lest Innocent Blood Be Shed and the documentary, Weapons of the Spirit, to discuss how they could help his Collège Cévenol in Le Chambon-sur-Lignon.

In 1947, the Sangrees began assisting the school—which had been set up on a shoestring in 1938 to help children of clergy, peasants and refugees—by establishing the American Friends of the College Cévenol to raise money and launch work camps where Northfield and Mount Hermon School students and faculty participated year after year. Among the NMH volunteers there was Richard Unsworth, who later became headmaster.

As for Cummington, the refugee hostel played an important role in the changing attitudes of some townspeople.

Sangree's granddaughter, Connie Talbot, was born two years after the release of *The Cummington Story*.

"When I was a kid, it was big thing what my grandfather had done," she recalls, even though she couldn't appreciate the implications until she grew older.

Although her grandfather's lifelong goal of "making connections" was controversial in Cummington, where today she is a potter married to the pastor of the West Cummington church, she says, "It was an experience of welcoming difference and 'the other' into your community."

"It was a great education," Gowdy recalls. "So much had been hidden from us. For those people to be suddenly thrown into a New England town was hard."

She has spoken about the film at some of the Cummington Historical Society's annual showings.

"It took me years to understand what they were going through," Gowdy says. "They hid it from us. It wasn't that easy to live together over there. They weren't used to the close circumstances. There were so many pressures on them. Their guard had to be up."

Reflecting on the air of suspicion in this country, particularly after the September 11 terrorist attacks, she questions how the same refugee situation in a small town would square today.

"I wonder how open we'd be."

One special memory stands out for Gowdy from when she was fourteen: one of the refugees she knew, a Mr. Greenbaum, asked her to borrow a recording of Beethoven's Ninth Symphony from the Pittsfield High School library. He sat in their living room with the girl and her mother, their wind-up Victrola playing the ten-inch recordings. She remembers him with eyes closed and tears streaming down his face during the final movement.

"You can only imagine what he heard."

**Cummington refugees**

# Distinguished Cummington Guests

## April 30, 2005 sidebar

*Although the dozens of refugees who came to Cummington were strangers here, their notoriety in their native Germany and Austria was striking. This story provides added understanding of who some of these exiles were, and how they went on from their safe haven here. Of nearly fifty World War II refugees hand-picked by Reverend Carl Sangree for Cummington Hostel, none was better known locally than Gustav Wolf.*

A painter and graphic artist who'd attended and then taught at the Academy of Fine and Applied Arts in Karlsruhe, Germany, Wolf had published books of illustrations and watercolors and exhibited his works in Cologne, Berlin, and Heidelberg. After 1933, he traveled to Switzerland, Italy, and Greece and completed more than two thousand drawings and watercolors of classical ruins.

Associated with a group known as Die Pforte which was trying to preserve Germany's cultural heritage but was portrayed by Hitler as "un-German," Wolf was forced to leave Germany with his wife in 1938. He arrived three years later in Cummington.

At the Cummington Press, Wolf illustrated the publisher's edition of The Book of Job, selected as one of the fifty most important books of 1944 by the American Institution of Graphic Arts.

From 1945 until his death in 1947, Wolf taught at Northfield School for Girls. He turned down an invitation to become director of Karlsruhe's arts museum, according to Gertraud Gutzmann, a professor at Smith College in Northampton.

In 1955, the Boston Public Library featured an exhibit of Wolf's works. In addition to a collection in Karlsruhe, the University of Texas has some seven hundred of his volumes and two hundred periodicals and pamphlets containing his work.

In Cummington, Wolf enjoyed the countryside, which resembled his home in southwestern Germany along with writers Paul Amann and Jacob Picard, said Gutzmann, who published an essay last year on Amann and the other exiles.

"Amman, Picard, and Wolf did what most Europeans do—they loved to take walks," Gutzmann said. "On Saturdays and Sundays, locals would be staring at them, surprised they'd be taking walks."

At Greenwood Music Camp, they listened to music and then visited a cafe on the road to Plainfield. "They would have coffee and cakes and would be surprised that no one was there except them and the Smith College girls waitressing," Gutzmann said. "It was a sign of a culture they had so loved yet seemed incomplete and not lived. They were sort of actors on an empty stage."

With a recommendation from German writer Thomas Mann, Amann arrived at the hostel in March 1942 and took a job at a sawmill shoveling sawdust.

A Czech-born Jew educated in Vienna, Prague, and Grenoble, Amann was a teacher of French and German and wrote translations of Italian poetry and essays on Goethe. A friend of Hermann Hesse and Nobel laureate Romain Rolland, he wrote a 1934 book, "Tradition and World Crisis," that contrasted German and French culture. The Nazis burned it.

At Cummington, Amann worked hard to translate his book into English. After teaching French and German to US soldiers at Ohio's

Kenyon College in 1943, Amann was hired to teach French part-time at Mount Hermon School for Boys in Northfield from 1944 until 1946 when he was asked to surrender his job to returning veterans. He went on to teach at Champlain College in Plattsburgh, New York.

An Austrian insurance broker, Werner Koenigsberger arrived in Cummington with his wife in September 1940 and bought a house where they set up a shop that sold their decoupage crafts.

Among other refugees passing through the hostel:

- Picard, a German lawyer turned poet and fiction writer who stayed at the hostel for six months in 1942, is the author of The Marked One, a 1936 work describing the lives of Jews in rural Germany. He taught at Columbia University, and in 1958 returned to Europe. Picard's works and personal papers in German, English, Yiddish, Dutch, and French are at the Leo Baeck Institute Center for Jewish History in New York. He was the Cummington hostel's gardener.
- Paul Frank, a Viennese lawyer, became a church choral director then music department head at Wittenberg College in Ohio.
- Hans "Hugo" Kallman, who had been editor of Germany's Frankfurter Zeitung newspaper, arrived in Cummington in June 1941 and began making wooden bowls. New York's Georg Jensen agreed to sell them exclusively when Sangree and Kallman visited the Fifth Avenue retailer with two burlap sacks filled with bowls. The store agreed to get him a house in Nyack, New York, and care for him as long as he agreed to produce bowls for them.
- Julius Boehm, who arrived in autumn 1940, had been on the Olympic Ski Team in Austria and began teaching the children of Cummington and Smith, Yale, and Amherst students. He moved to Cambridge and then Seattle, where he worked for a mattress factory.
- Painter Paul Weighardt and his wife, sculptor Nelli Barr, emigrated to New York by way of Russia, Japan, and 'Mexico, arriving in Cummington in March 1941. Injured during World War I, Weighardt was made speechless by the shock of World War II, but after three months at the hostel, he began to draw, paint, and talk. Weighardt taught from 1950 to 1954 at the Art Institute of Chicago, where his students included the pop sculptor Claes Oldenburg.

- Johannes Hans Gaides, a German agricultural economist, was the first hostel arrival in May 1940. He went on to study at Harvard University.
- Michael and Stephen Gottschalk, ten and twelve, arrived in June 1940, and were later reunited with their parents and moved to Heath that August.
- Emily Ott, a landscape painter, arrived in this country in 1938 with her daughter Susan. She worked as a housekeeper at the hostel, then worked in the dormitories at the Northfield School for Girls while her daughter attended. It was such a difficult position to be in, recalls Cummington resident Gloria Gowdy. "Her husband got rid of her because she was a Jew."

The refugees also included several physicians, who had to be recertified. Among them were Kurt Jellinek of Salzburg, Austria, whose wife worked as a hostess at the hostel while he interned at Holyoke Hospital and George Beer, who went on to work at a hospital in Boston.

photo by Peter MacDonald

David Kaynor fiddling at May Day celebration, Montague Center

# The Music Community's Guiding Star

### January 10, 2019

*I began contra dancing in college, where our dance master from Maine told us about Ralph Page and other legendary callers. I couldn't have imagined landing in a contra dance capital like Greenfield. The Kaynor family had already become synonymous with fiddling and calling around the region, but it was cousin David who settled in Montague and created a well-connected community of fiddling, calling, dancing, and ritual celebrating. Sadly, David passed away as we completed work on* Good Will & Ice Cream. *He remains beloved by many.*

*In the ten months between the two interviews reflected here, David went from being able to speak with me—although much more slowly than in past conversations—to having to type responses, leaving his computer to speak for him. A year and a half later, when his finger muscles deteriorated due to ALS, David had a tracheotomy and a feeding tube inserted and began using an eye-gaze device to communicate by spell-out messages with eye movements. Incredibly, he even used eye-gaze technology to continue writing fiddle tunes.*

*In 2021, David was honored by the Country Dance and Song Society as the recipient of its 2021 Lifetime Contribution Award "in recognition for his enormous contributions as a dance community organizer, musician, caller, and mentor to generations."*

———

While alternating contradance couples move up and down the lines at Greenfield's Guiding Star Grange on weekends, David Kaynor inspires other musicians sharing the stage as he acts as caller or plays fiddle.

He has also become its grounding, guiding spirit.

Kaynor, 70, has been a staple of the nationally known Greenfield dances for nearly forty years as well as a central figure in building community around traditional music, dance, and ritual. He's also credited with keeping Grange halls in Greenfield, Montague, and beyond alive and swinging.

"He is an institution around here," says Alice Yang of Sunderland, who first met Kaynor when she was a novice fiddler about ten years ago and wanted to find other people to make music with.

Yang is also co-founder of the Fiddle Orchestra of western Massachusetts—one of two such ensembles led by Kaynor, who also plays a key role in a twenty-three-year-old Monday night open jam in Montague Center. Like at his pioneering contra dances, he's used it to mentor musicians and dancers who are just getting their fingers or feet warmed up.

"There are so many people who play this kind of music around the Pioneer Valley," acknowledges Yang, "but he's the force stronger than anybody who's kept it alive and fresh."

## Teaching Himself

Unlike his Amherst cousins, Cammy and Van Kaynor, who also play the instrument thought in some circles to be a violin, David Kaynor is a self-taught fiddler who's continued to feed the fire of traditional music and dance in Greenfield, his adopted hometown of Montague Center, and beyond.

"I grew up in a family that was really good at harmonizing," offers the Montague musician, whose father sang barbershop-style harmonies to pass the time washing and drying dishes with his six siblings.

Kaynor learned to play trumpet while growing up in Wilbraham, then also picked up mandolin, banjo, and guitar. He taught himself fiddle with help from the Arm and Hammer String Band while living in Burlington, Vermont, and went on to play at social events.

He joined his family's Petersham dances and then Cammy's popular Friday night Northfield dances as part of the family's Fourgone Conclusions dance band, with his Uncle Ed on piano. The entire family has had a profound, lasting impact on the contra dance revival up and down the Pioneer Valley.

When a dance was launched in Greenfield a couple of years later, he fiddled and soon began calling in a calming, rambling, down-home style.

"That was a real hot time," recalls Kaynor, who moved to Montague Center in 1982 from Belchertown. "I just learned calling by throwing myself in. I'd been watching Cammy and Ralph Sweet . . . and I'd also been dancing a lot, so I had role models with examples of things to do and not to do."

When the Northfield dance ended in the early 1980s, remembers Cammy, who's since moved to the Boston area, "Greenfield was poised to take off, and indeed it became and still is a mecca of contra dancing in western Massachusetts with the heart and soul of David Kaynor in its foundation."

Kaynor had become so good at fiddling that he accompanied the Green Mountain Volunteers dance group on its European tour in 1978. At a week-long festival in Bulgaria, he bonded with a Swedish folklore group and visited its members the following year to learn Swedish fiddling and folk dance.

"I liked a lot of different types of music—Irish, Scottish, Quebeçois. But having a group of friends to connect with the music, that was really big. The social experience of the music was a major driver."

The Swedish immersion would solidify over the years—through repeated visits and teaching at contra dances and instrumental sessions—into a connection not only for Kaynor but for scores of fiddlers, dancers, and even weavers like Shelburne's Becky Ashenden.

"When I play music with David, both Swedish and contra," says Van Kaynor, now a Suzuki violin teacher in the Amherst village of Cushman, "he has this uncanny ability to improvise a third part, a second harmony. David has basically watched and learned and become quite proficient as a self-taught musician."

### A New Challenge

"I feel scared. I feel despair. And at times, I feel denial: 'This must be something else,'" Kaynor says slowly, seated in his living room one recent afternoon.

Kaynor was recently diagnosed with Amyotrophic Lateral Sclerosis, ALS, also known as Lou Gehrig's disease, the incurable motor neuron disease that weakens muscles—especially those associated with speaking, swallowing, and breathing.

He began noticing pain in his shoulder, hip, and back nearly a year and a half ago. The problem was diagnosed at the time as polymyalgia rheumatica, and his doctor prescribed Prednisone, resulting in temporary improvement. Then, last April, "I started realizing I had to work harder to not sound like I was slurring my words. People started remarking on it," Kaynor says.

In June, Kaynor—an avid runner—noticed that when he was out running, "I would feel my airway was closing up. My muscles were fine. I was exhaling fine. But breathing in, it felt like the airway became a one-way valve.

"I've also lost more and more resonance, tone and projection. Speaking is getting harder and harder."

Pausing occasionally between words and sometimes even between syllables, he lets drop that he may have called his last dance.

"I haven't made a final decision, but it is so hard for me. My lips and tongue have definitely changed. There are things I can't do anymore. Playing? I'll see how long I can go. My hands do feel different, but it's hard to say what that actually means."

Less than a year later, his ALS has made speech so difficult that Kaynor can respond to questions only by typing responses that his laptop computer vocalizes.

"My playing has deteriorated," Kaynor types shortly after an October 2019 Greenfield contra dance where he was presented with a Massachusetts House of Representatives citation for his "steadfast allegiance to traditional music and dance, mentoring individuals and building community in western Massachusetts and beyond."

He adds, "I don't have the unconscious muscle control in each hand that I used to have. So my playing takes more concentration than simply playing notes in time and in tune. I feel like it's way more work. I have to focus more on the physical act of playing, so I don't get the emotional experience of it. What I miss is the emotional immersion."

Kaynor also "says" he's become more distracted, even though he can still recall hundreds of tunes, including dozens of his own compositions.

He's lost so much muscle mass that his fiddle can't rest on his shoulder the way it has for the past fifty years.

"Holding the instrument in playing position is a new and increasingly challenging task," so he's curtailed practicing fiddle "mostly because it's discouraging."

Kaynor's "found some encouragement" playing a few recent dances, like the recent Greenfield one with his "Back Row Band."

"But at the same time it makes the prospect of losing the ability to play with and for these people all the more troubling. I'm filled with gratitude and a sense of accomplishment.

"On the other hand, it adds to the grief that comes with the feeling the end is in sight."

## Music, Dance, Community

Whether or not it's the end of calling or playing for Kaynor, it's clear he's already played a lasting impact on the Pioneer Valley.

"The thing I think David's done best in his life is he's encouraged hundreds of people who probably never really saw themselves as up-and-coming musicians," says Susan Secco of Northfield.

Secco was encouraged to hone her piano skills to play at dances, where she found Kaynor welcoming to everyone.

"There was always an open-door policy on stage," she says. "He's had a mission, trying hard to break down barriers."

Ray Sebold of Montague has known Kaynor for decades as a dancer and as a regular at the thirty-five-year-old Montague May Day celebration where the fiddle master led the grand opening fiddling procession and Maypole dances. He says, "One of the things David has been very clear on is that he doesn't like an exclusivity to dancing. From the get-go, he was always against an 'experienced' dance for more advanced dancers."

In fact, the fifth-Friday newcomers dance starts an hour early as a free session to encourage not only beginners but also more experienced dancers willing to join them as Kaynor walks them through basics, avoiding the kind of complicated choreography and tunes that he feels may discourage those starting out.

"It's a very generous thing," Sebold observes. He also points to Kaynor's decision to become a Guiding Star Grange member, encouraging musicians and dancers to also join when the 145-year-old agricultural organization was struggling.

A fundraising contra dance spearheaded by Kaynor and others in 1996 raised sixty-three hundred dollars toward renovations, recalls Sebold, who served as Guiding Star president then.

Kaynor remembers getting "a lot of sideways looks" from old-timers when he joined the Montague Grange in 1988 after facing resistance from members to scheduling regular contra dances there.

A non-profit group he spearheaded purchased the Montague Common Hall in 2013, where he'd been calling dances since moving to town. It's been the focus of that group's continuing efforts to renovate it as a community centerpiece.

Becky Hollingsworth, a longtime Montague friend and piano player at some of Kaynor's dances, says that in music, dance, and community-building efforts, he embodies the ethic, "If we want to keep a resource, we've got to do something."

"He sets the example and demystifies it and begins encouraging people to do it," she adds.

"If I hadn't joined and some others hadn't," Kaynor acknowledges, "both Grange halls probably would have been sold. Whether dancing could have continued under new ownership is hard to say."

## Dances for Everyone

Van Kaynor explains that his cousin "is so committed to the community aspect that he won't compromise that in order to get more people to come" to his dances as he refuses to appeal to polished performers where sit-in musicians feel shunned and beginners may be intimidated.

"He's so inclusive. There's been more and more expectation for the music to be rehearsed, so it's not as spontaneous. In the old days, we just made up melodies at the dance, on the fly."

At many dances, "anybody can take part—any income, any age. So you may see a nine-year-old dancing with an eighty-year-old," Van Kaynor says. Dancers are welcomed as beginners or veterans, couples or singles.

At all such celebrations, you'll find David Kaynor inviting everyone to join in with whatever they have to offer.

"Through him, I've had so many opportunities to play—at sessions, dances, May Days, farmers markets, and other events," says fiddler

47

Donna Francis of Montague. "He's been a very important part of my musical life. And the tunes he knows—hundreds! His memory is remarkable not only for tunes, but he is the only dance caller I know who never uses any notes."

Asked about his cousin David's role, Cammy Kaynor says, "I feel heartened that so many people took up the vision and preserved not just the superficial aspects but the deeper and the visceral reasons for having traditions like these. It would not have been possible without the exceptional leaders like David, who built communities like the Guiding Star Grange dancing public, the Montague Center activities, and similar core communities across the country."

Kaynor's left a legacy across the country both as a fiddle instructor and dance instructor in workshops and as a caller at countless dance camps.

"When you go to a festival somewhere and you find an impromptu crowd of fiddlers chugging away on 'Fisher's Hornpipe' with harmonies and improvisations coloring the swelling sound of the melody, there is a good chance you will find David in the middle of the crowd prompting, encouraging, smiling, and giving it his all," Cammy Kaynor says. "That is who David is, that is what inspires us. And that is what we all need."

The possibility to grow community dances, Cammy adds, "is all the more possible because of people like David, who have set the seed in so many places."

"He's made music accessible to novices like me," says Yang, "not only because of his musical abilities and his teaching and leading skills, but also because of his big open heart and his great sense of humor. He's definitely doing it out of love, because 'community music makes the world a better place' seems to be his life mission.

Kaynor, for whom time may be running out, acknowledges the timelessness of the music he plays and teaches—including dozens of original fiddle tunes—has played a core role in the sense of place where it's taken hold.

Kaynor has connected musicians, dancers, and others through tunes he's composed, played, and taught, many of whom have come, gone and returned, sometimes years later.

"It's sort of like the community's like a river delta where there are all these different branches of the flow," he reflects.

"Dance is one of the branches. And one of the nice things is that people can take side trips out of it for however long—a month, a year, a decade—and then they can flow back in."

**Martha and Waitstill Sharp**

## The Sharps' War

### April 3, 2013 • September 10, 2016

*I'd known Waitstill Sharp as a guest minister at the Unitarian-Universalist Church in my early years in Greenfield. Because of his commanding, serious presence, I wasn't surprised years later when I read an account of his heroic work during World War II.*

-----

The heroic story of a former Greenfield minister and his wife who traveled in 1939 to rescue hundreds of refugees from Czechoslovakia and France on the brink of war "reads like a spy novel." It's the subject of a new Ken Burns documentary.

*Defying the Nazis: The Sharps' War* features Tom Hanks and Marina Goldman of Montague as the voices of Martha and Waitstill Sharp, who undertook their heroic mission defying the Nazis decades before he moved to Greenfield with his second wife.

The Sharps were honored by Yad Vashem, Israel's Holocaust Memorial, as members of its Righteous of the Nations in 2005 and 2006.

Built on a 2012 documentary researched by their grandson, Artemis Joukowsky III, whose book about them was published by Beacon Press, the Burns film was previewed at the White House and shown on PBS.

Sharp, a thirty-seven-year-old minister at the Wellesley Hills Unitarian Society, and his thirty-three-year-old wife, Martha, a social worker who'd worked at Chicago's Hull House, were involved in social and political issues at the church when they received a phone call in January 1939 from the head of the American Unitarian Association. He asked them to travel to Czechoslovakia to lead an emergency relief mission.

Leaving their two young children behind safely in Wellesley, the Sharps arrived in Prague the following month. It was just a few weeks before Germany, which had annexed part of Czechoslovakia in 1938, took control of the capital and the rest of the country. The Sharps interviewed more than 3,500 endangered Jews and gentiles, according to three Keene State College professors who played a role in researching the film.

Over the next seven months, Sharp also organized an underground escape path for the refugees' money to various English, French, and Swiss banks that would aid the Jewish intellectuals, writers, political dissidents, and union organizers.

The couple helped individuals and families by giving them money to help them survive in countries where they had no work, no family, and few assets. The Sharps also helped refugees escape Czechoslovakia by connecting them with employers and sponsors abroad.

Pursued by Nazi police and Gestapo patrols, the Sharps had their offices ransacked and faced arrest for aiding refugees. They left Prague in August 1939, the day after hearing their arrest was imminent.

They left with the Nazis at their heels.

"On the night the Nazis entered Prague in early March 1939, the Sharps burned their notes and kept no further records," according to the Unitarian Universalist Service Committee." Their personal peril increased when the Gestapo closed down their office at the end of July, but the Sharps were committed to completing their mission.

"Waitstill left Prague in early August for a conference in Switzerland," the service committee continues, "but was prevented from returning to Czechoslovakia. Martha departed from Prague alone a week later, learning only afterward that she had escaped capture by the Gestapo by one day."

"I found a taxi in the early darkness," Martha Sharp detailed in one later account, "and noting that the driver had a companion in the front seat, gave an address which was near but not actually the one which was my destination.

"The 'extra cargo' tried to engage me in conversation," Martha continued, "but I parried his questions. Arriving at the place, I hastily paid the driver and walked around the corner, hiding in the first doorway to watch and see whether I was being followed.

"The 'companion' came around the same corner, looked up the street, down an alley or two, and then walked along the street," she wrote. "The driver honked. My heart raced as I realized that my follower must be a Gestapo agent. I flattened myself against the entrance and, in the darkness, he walked right by and then headed back toward the cab."

After briefly returning to Wellesley, the couple accepted a mission from the newly formed Unitarian Service Committee to return to war-torn Europe in June 1940. There, they assisted in setting up and staffing the committee's office in Lisbon, a final European refuge city for many escaping the Nazi regime.

The Sharps spent most of 1940 working in Vichy-controlled France, where Martha organized delivery of thirteen tons of milk products to feed starving infants and arranged for transport of twenty-nine European children to this country. Together, the couple helped hundreds of intellectuals, Jews, and other at-risk populations flee the country.

"The Sharps' work was divided, as it would be for the following six years, between relief and emigration assistance," according to the Service Committee. "Much of their activity involved individual cases, but on one occasion Martha escorted thirty-five refugees—among them journalists, political leaders, and two children whose parents had committed suicide—to England and on another arranged for a group of children to leave in cooperation with the organization British Kinderaction.

Yad Vashem describes how the Sharps, who sought ways to help Jewish and non-Jewish fugitives escape, learned that the world-famous German-Jewish anti-Nazi author Lion Feuchtwanger needed to be helped out of France immediately with his wife. Both Feuchtwangers were on a Nazi extermination list. In addition to personally escorting the couple to safety across the Pyrenees, Sharp also convinced Otto Meyerhof, a Jewish Nobel Prize recipient, to escape.

Throughout the long trip to the Spanish-Portuguese border, Waitstill watched over Feuchtwanger, keeping inquisitive fellow travelers at a safe distance to lessen the danger of his disclosure to Spanish police and the risk of his being returned to Vichy French hands.

Yad Vashem named the Sharps as members of its Righteous of the Nations in 2005 and honored them in a ceremony the following year. The only other American among twenty-one thousand non-Jews who has been so honored is Emergency Rescue Committee head Varian Fry, who worked closely with the Sharps and has been described as "The American Schindler."

"It was the greatest episode of my life," Sharp told *Recorder* reporter Irmarie Jones of that wartime era in a 1976 interview in Greenfield, where he moved in 1972 after serving parishes in Iowa, Michigan, and then Petersham. "I had a ringside seat to history." By then, Sharp had divorced Martha and remarried.

"The story of the Sharps reads like a spy novel, but it's all true," writes Burns in his forward to Joukowsky's 255-page book. "It explores that rare level of character—selfless sacrifice for the greater good—that we have always admired and celebrated in this country. The Sharps saw there was a job to be done and, quite simply, did it."

Unitarians in Greenfield—where Sharp moved with his second wife, Monica, in 1972 after serving parishes in Iowa, Michigan, and then Petersham—never heard the story of his earlier adventure, according to Ann Howard, whose husband, Stephen, had been minister where Sharp led occasional services.

"He was never famous when he was with us," she says. "It was in the background."

One Greenfield churchgoer, Joan Benneyan, recalls the minister's humble quality, reading bedtime stories to her children when he was at her home for dinner and revealing another side when the fire department responded to a chimney fire during a Christmas Eve party at their house:

"Well, he thought that was wonderful, and afterward, he asked, 'Could I get a ride home on your truck?' He was like a little boy. It was a riot, that this very worldly, intelligent man still had that side to him."

Sharp died in 1984. Martha Sharp died fifteen years later.

Even Joukowsky—who explains that his grandfather "viewed the story as divulging the secrets of rescue" and "was very angry about others who were kind of bragging about their exploits"—didn't learn about it until, as a high-school freshmen assigned to write a social studies paper on moral courage, was advised by his mother that her parents had a story to tell.

The Burns documentary was also shown at the United States Holocaust Memorial Museum in Washington, DC, following the White House special screening as part of the Obama administration's focus on the Syrian refugee crisis.

"This is our watershed moment," says Joukowsky. "It's unbelievable how relevant it is. I think PBS has chosen this film very specifically to make a statement about humanizing the face of refugees and saying every one of them is a human being, every one deserves everything that we believe in in this country."

Joukowsky had begun researching his grandmother's papers soon after her death in 1999—first about the people the Sharps had been unable to rescue. Documents relating to the people rescued had been burned to avoid leaving a trace.

"At first we started to archive them," he says, "and before you knew it, we had this amazing history of American rescue during the Holocaust, which no one ever knew anything about."

The papers helped to document the Sharps' nomination for Yad Vashem, and its acceptance in 2006 led him to begin work on his own documentary, *Two Who Dared*. Goldman, who'd heard the heroic story years earlier from Joukowsky's mother, was cast as Martha Sharp and read from her memoir.

Joukowsky began working with the educational organization Facing History and Ourselves to convey the importance of the Sharps' humanitarian work. But to reach a wider audience, he sought out Burns, who'd graduated from Hampshire College a decade earlier, in 1975, and whom he knew from fund-raising at the college.

Burns originally rejected Joukowsky's request to "help get this ready for PBS," says Goldman, "but Artemis, being the persistent, pragmatic person he is, kept trying, and we sat with him in Walpole, New Hampshire, and watched it together.

"And Ken says, 'Oh, my God—I'm going to work on this with you.'"

Burns, who went from being an adviser to a producer to director on the film, made changes throughout.

"It was a different film, with many of the same interviews," Joukowsky says. "He used all the best parts of the old film, but we changed everything. What you learn working with Ken Burns is that filmmaking is all in the editing room. We've really allowed Martha and Waitstill to narrate their own stories. One thing Ken did was really make it a human story, a love story, not just a story of rescues but of the personal lives in the rescues."

Erwin Staub, a University of Massachusetts emeritus psychology professor who recently authored *The Roots of Goodness and Resistance to Evil,* says the Sharps' story represents great moral courage, but in addition, "great determination and the willingness to make very substantial sacrifices, for example by leaving their children behind.

"We seem now to be in a variety of ways on a downward course," Staub continues, "with people getting more and more critical of each other with expressions of hostility towards various other groups, and here were these people willing to put themselves out so intensely for 'the other'. They saw the humanity in 'the other' and the great danger to 'the other' and were willing to do whatever was within their power to protect people and save lives. We desperately need this."

"One can only manage a miracle every so often," Martha Sharp wrote. "But a series of miracles can happen when many people become concerned and are willing to act at the right time."

**Deb Habib with Vanessa Lynch and Malcolm Hall, around 2009**

# Food Project Takes Root

## July 10, 2012 • June 26, 2018

*Deb Habib and her husband, Ricky Baruc, are highly committed, imaginative and enterprising friends who have promoted organic agricultural and sustainable energy practices not just for customers who can afford it, but universally. This combines two of numerous stories I've written about their work.*

————

The tops of Asian greens, kale, and Swiss chard tower over the heads of the smallest of the fifteen or so kids at Educare child care center in Orange, but those tots don't shrink from their vegetable garden.

Four-year-old Zoe McNamara comes running when she hears Deborah Habib say "radish" and immediately yanks at the root vegetable from the corner of the raised-bed Grow-Food-Everywhere garden Habib has planted.

"I love radishes," the girl says to another child in the group as she looks at the tiny red vegetable at the end of the stalk she's just pulled from the bounty of spinach, peppers, cucumbers, and greens growing beside the parking lot.

The idea is simple: When parents come to get their children, those same kids encourage them to take home the vegetables they've helped to grow.

All around the nine-town North Quabbin region, these "Grow Gardens Everywhere for Food and Justice" are feeding families and other institutional centers with the help of a two-year, ninety-five-thousand-dollar grant from the state in order "to promote preventive care and reduce health care disparities." They're a project of Habib's Seeds of Solidarity nonprofit organization.

At Educare's "kinder garden"—one of more than twenty gardens along with raised-bed gardens at Wheeler Memorial Library, Orange Innovation Center, and West River Health Center—fifty-one children, parents, and other volunteers turned out in May to assemble precut boards and fill raised beds with 240 gallons of a compost-and-loam mixture and seeds. The grant paid for all materials.

Desiree Malcolm, 13, helped drill together boards of the raised beds in May and enjoys watching the produce as it "keeps getting bigger and bigger." She first got interested in gardening as a third-grader at Dexter Park Elementary School, where Seeds of Solidarity set up a garden years ago.

Habib, who drives off in her red vegetable-oil-burning diesel Golf from the childcare center to one of sixteen homes where families have been given wood-frame gardens, got the idea for the project ten years ago and jumped on the opportunity to apply when state funding became available.

The Grow-Food-Everywhere message is that all communities need to become more food strong," explains Habib, who points to the project's gardens in the front yards of several houses as she drives by. "Individuals in our community need to reclaim the power of food—not only of having local food from farmers but reclaiming our own right to grow, produce and eat our own food."

That includes relearning skills that make people more self-reliant and "food resilient," especially in Orange and Athol where per capita income is ranked among the lowest of the state's 351 communities.

"There's a lot of hungry people in our community," Habib says.

## Seeds of Leadership

But the Grow-Food-Everywhere gardens are just one of Habib's crops to nourish people and their souls.

Another is Seeds of Leadership, which offers teens room to grow. The program's SOL garden where kale, salad greens, scallions, and tomatoes grow, also has enriched the lives of its more than 450 participants over twenty years as they've learned to tend the garden and one another, building structures as well as relationships.

Offered through Habib's and husband Ricky Baruc's nonprofit educational foundation, the afterschool program each afternoon and during summer has workshops on cooking and ecology plus cultural events and community-building exercises.

"This is for young people who are interested in a positive experience of community," says Habib. "It's nice if they're interested in gardening and the great outdoors, but that comes. Mostly we're looking for young people who are interested in being part of a positive community and gaining leadership skills that they can extend outward into the community and continue in their own lives."

Habib, who met Baruc when they worked at Cape Cod's New Alchemy Institute, visits science classes at local high schools each spring to talk about sustainable gardening and green energy and to recruit volunteers for the twenty-week program.

"I was really trying to get into gardening at the time," recalls third-year SOL member Olivia Parnanen, 17, who first heard Habib speak in her chemistry class. "But then I realized it's . . . like a little community: no matter what, everyone loves you and you're accepted by all, and it's best to be yourself here."

"It taught me about being honest in a lot of different ways: how to be honest with yourself, with who you are, and what your abilities are, in what you do," says Zach Gordon, a 2011 Mahar graduate who went on to attend Greenfield Community College, get a sociology degree and then a master's in sustainable food systems.

"The hook for me was having a group of people I could come to every week and grow with them," Gordon says, "and thinking about these bigger issues, about living in a world where people don't have to starve.

"And getting affirmation that I do have a part in this and I can help change it," he continues, "when the world outside you is always saying, 'No, you can't help it much. Especially coming from Orange, where I watched so many of my peers crumble to the wayside because generational poverty has a strong hold on people."

Each SOL session begins with an opening circle, and at today's gathering as teens pass around bags of crackers and cookies, Habib asks for volunteers to serve at the Orange community meal, where she plans to bring a garlic-pesto salad and stir-fried bok choy with carrots.

"Part of the magic of the group is that the kids come with a diversity of life experiences," she says. "Some have been successful in school and society, some have struggled more, some have harder lives or less so. But the experience of just being here together and engaged in authentic work transcends all of that."

Four-year volunteer Micky McKinley, who brings years of experience as a Hitchcock Center nature educator, says,

"They feel safe and accepted. They don't feel judged, and it changes their lives. We do all these programs and eat together and make food together, and many of these kids open up about their feelings, and this is a place where they feel okay doing that."

"I've learned to take opportunities whenever you're given them," says Monty Duprey, 14. "I've learned there really are a bunch of different plants and different ways to prepare them and that making these plants is a lot harder than it seems . . . But everyone here's just so kind and caring. They feel like family."

## Food Justice

Back in town, Habib's tomato-colored veggiemobile plugs through neighborhoods, and she points out new raised-bed oases of veggies that have sprung up, no doubt inspired by her Grow-Food-Everywhere gardens.

It's a popular misconception, she says, "that poor people don't care about wanting fresh food, they just want junk. That's so not true! Everybody still wants to feed their kids good, fresh food."

In her attempt to fight hunger and help kids in the community be well-nourished, "This is our approach to food justice, if you will, and increasing access to fresh food."

The project, involving SOL teens cutting and preparing the boards with soy-based stain before helping install them for people with more than a cubic yard of compost, also provides families with a way to spend time together "in this age of excessive screen time engaged in a really positive activity that's about self-determination."

All that's required for the families to join the program is a statement that it's hard for them to afford to buy the vegetables they want for their families, along with a commitment to maintain the gardens.

And if some nonprofit organizations try to spread their reach to broader areas, Habib says Seeds of Solidarity—which she and her husband launched seventeen years ago—has its roots firmly planted in these North Quabbin communities.

As Seeds of Solidarity works to close the loop between helping area schools and young families grow their own food while sharing resilience with needy people in the community, "We keep going deeper and stronger."

## Gardens Everywhere

In fact, Rick Innes of Clearview Composting in Orange, which provided Habib with fourteen tons of a compost-loam mix for the project, reports that he's sold nearly that same amount to other people who have seen Grow-Food-Everywhere gardens, well, everywhere.

"You just start seeing gardens around, all over the community, and it kind of becomes the norm to see them," says Habib, like a latter-day Appleseed.

One of those new copycat gardens is across the street from the Athol house where Kirby Cox and her three sons—Caleb, Connor, and Camden—survey the bumper crop in their own Grow-Food-Everywhere garden.

"I thought it was a really a good option," offers Cox, who along with her husband, David, were both involved in Habib's SOL Garden program ten years ago as teens. "The kids are really picky eaters, and I thought this would be a really good way to get them involved. They'll eat it if they're doing the whole process, which is really working for the two younger ones."

Two-year-old Camden, she says, "loves to be hands-on, playing in the dirt. If we're out and about, I ask what he wants to do when we get home, and it's the garden. It's been really fun, and as it's getting bigger, they're getting more excited."

Eight-year-old Caleb and four-year-old Connor say they like watering the garden with David in the early morning, and Caleb points out how the little veggie patch is coming along: cucumbers, broccoli, carrots, lettuce, eggplant, and "basils."

His mother—whom Habib has a photo of as a teen farmer at the Dexter Park School garden, with Caleb in her womb and a young Desiree Malcolm at her side—says that first experience gardening is what got her interested in eating vegetables—something she's trying to pass on to her sons.

## Extended Season

"We've only gotten to pick chard and lettuce so far, and they tried it," says Cox, who wasn't able to garden when the couple lived in apartments before they bought their house from the foreclosure market a couple of years ago. "There are very limited options—just tacos and spaghetti every day. But this is really nice to have something to do, and they want to eat it because they did it. It's been awesome that they're finally interested in eating okay."

Toward the end of summer, Habib says all of the families who gathered in March to begin thinking about what they wanted to plant and how to do it will come together for a dinner at her farm where they'll be given metal hoops, heavy-duty plastic for a greenhouse-like season extender, and more seeds that may take their gardens all the way to the end of the year.

That, says Cox, is what got her husband excited at the prospect of joining the program.

At Wheeler Library, wooden benches face the donated garden, where anyone can pick a vegetable and munch while reading. At the health center, dieticians and nurse practitioners can show patients exactly where in the five gardens they can find green, leafy vegetables recommended for them. At the Orange Innovation Center, three gardens provide food for the Orange Food Pantry and gardening therapy at the Center for Human Development.

"Somebody says, 'But what if somebody takes things?'" remarks Habib. "Great! Take kale, take tomatoes!"

**Ken Burns**

# Cinematic Historian

### February 27, 2010

*Ken Burns, who helped create his Florentine Films production company while a student at Hampshire College in Amherst, has had a profound impact on popularizing documentary films. I felt I share the same deep curiosity and interest in telling stories that matter to people as this prolific film producer just up the river, so I was inspired to visit him for this interview. Since this was written, Burns has helped create documentaries on the Vietnam War, country music, Jackie Robinson, and* The Sharps War, *the subject of an earlier story in this book.*

—————

The focus for documentary filmmaker Ken Burns has historically been history itself.

Because of his Emmy Award-winning 1990 series on the Civil War and his 2007 series on World War II, his cinematic chronicles of jazz, baseball, Thomas Jefferson, and more, the filmmaker has been called the greatest documentarian of the day. In the words of the *Baltimore Sun's* David Zurawik, Burns "showed us a new way of looking at our collective past and ourselves."

Not surprisingly, Burns's own history has played a big part in development of his artistic vision. But that's only clear in retrospect, he says, while sitting behind a project-laden desk in the barn-top studio located behind his home in Walpole, New Hampshire.

"My very first memory is of my dad building a darkroom when I was two or three years old in the basement of our house."

"Very early on, I remember that early magic when you're in the darkroom with the eerie light and the pictures come up," he says, recalling times spent beside his amateur photographer dad in Brooklyn, then Delaware and Michigan. "Imagine what that was like for a kid."

## The Power of Image

The documentarian's father, Robert Kyle Burns, was a cultural anthropologist who took the family for the first year of Kenneth Lauren Burns's life in 1953 off to study the culture of Saint Veran, a French Alpine village.

Seeking documentation of that time, Burns reaches behind his desk where one of his ten golden Emmy Award trophies looks out like a ship's figurehead. From a bookcase that holds a bust of Abraham Lincoln gazing down, Burns pulls out an April 1959 edition of *National Geographic*. In it is an article by his father chronicling the trip to Saint Veran. Among several of Robert Burns's black-and-white photographs in the magazine is a photo of Ken Burns as a baby with the caption—"Kenny Burns takes lunch from mother's hand."

"This became a kind of iconic thing for me all my life," says Burns, dressed in jeans and sweater over his T-shirt, the wonder at the Alpine photos expressed in his voice. "I remember seeing him print these photographs."

An aspiring filmmaker, Burns was given an eight-millimeter movie camera for his seventeenth birthday in Ann Arbor, Michigan. And, according to one account, he used it to film an exposé of a nearby factory.

He made a "strange, fortuitous" choice in attending newly created Hampshire College in Amherst, where he graduated in 1975. His film teachers there were the legendary documentary still photographers Jerome Liebling and Elaine Mayes.

"They were uninterested in what I was interested in, the Hollywood route," says the barely bearded, fifty-six-year-old filmmaker. "Very shortly, I had all my molecules re-arranged and was wanting to make documentary films."

Burns, who returned to Hampshire College in 2009 to help dedicate the new Jerome Liebling Center for Film, Photography, and Video with a Ken Burns wing, recalls students screening their eight- and sixteen-millimeter projects in the same space where Liebling and Mayes displayed their iconic still images.

"Can you imagine what it was like for a nineteen-year-old to see the heroic, immortal pictures of cadavers that he took or heroic men working in the slaughterhouses or any of the pictures that he and she took at that time?" Burns asks. "They were just transformational."

"The power of an individual image—a still image—to convey complex information ... that's what I learned all my life. I think it was amplified at Hampshire, and then applied in what I've done. The DNA, the building block, of what we do, is still the image. We treat the old photographs as if they're live, and we treat the live cinematography as if they're paintings."

## Waking the Dead

If his father's influence as a cultural anthropologist—along with those Alpine images focused Burns on how he would later examine the societal dimensions of history, living with a mother who battled cancer during his childhood would profoundly affect the filmmaker's life's work.

"It took me until I was in my forties to put it all together," he says of the impact of his mother, Lyla Burns, the young biotechnician in that *National Geographic* photograph. "There was never a moment when she wasn't sick. I mean dying. From the time I was three on, I was immediately forced to confront her mortality and then, by six or seven, I was told she was going to die. Then, she died when I was a few months short of twelve, a hugely traumatic event." His father died in 2001.

Only in retrospect did a friend make clear the meaning of his creating historical documentaries. "Look what you do for a living: you wake the dead," Burns recalls. "Then he says, 'Who do you think you're really trying to wake up?'"

Burns's films stir voices from dusty diaries and letters. They juxtapose them with panning sepia-toned images so meticulously that Apple Computers dubbed the technique The Ken Burns Effect in its iPhoto and iMovie applications. For Burns, it's a way "to get inside a photograph and resurrect the time in which it was taken and trust that that may be the closest representation we have to the past," the filmmaker told a *PhotoJournalism* interviewer.

His genius for "getting inside" a historical photo and resurrecting the era and the moment in which it was taken was sparked by *Brooklyn Bridge,* a film he made after leaving Hampshire.

Made with Florentine Films and completed in 1981 *Brooklyn Bridge* was nominated for an Academy Award as best documentary.

"I was drawn to the story of it," he says of the landmark bridge. "But I realized, since it's pre-cinema, that the only way you were going to tell it was through still photography."

What the filmmaker soon learned, though, was that relying on still images for a motion picture wasn't limiting. It was as liberating as his Hampshire education had been.

"When you've got some footage of Babe Ruth running around the bases," Burns says, "the only thing you can really talk about is Babe Ruth running around the bases. But if you've got a beautiful portrait, a head shot of Babe Ruth, of which there are many spectacular ones, you can talk about him running around the bases. But you can also talk about his unhappy childhood on the Baltimore wharves, you can talk about his difficult off-the-field life—his problems with wives, money, and teammates—you can talk about his celebrity. You can see into a kind of soul."

Some documentary filmmakers have used re-creations to compensate for lack of historical film footage, but the most Burns has ever done is a segment of just a few minutes in his 1997 Lewis and Clark biography. Instead, he declares, "It is the (ability) of the individual image to present complex information without undue manipulation that I'm interested in."

## Bottom-up History

His approach is what's helped us become interested, as well.

"More Americans get their history from Ken Burns than any other source," the late historian Stephen Ambrose once observed.

Burns's series on national parks was watched by thirty-four million people, thirty-nine million watched *Civil War,* thirty-eight million watched *The War*, and forty-three million watched *Baseball*—"just the first time, not subsequent showings, not counting school showings nor DVD sales."

Growing up, Burns never even thought of history as his favorite subject. However, at Hampshire, where his first student project was a film on the 'living museum' Old Sturbridge Village, he realized "just intuitively, that there was this latent, untrained, absolute passion for American history."

The filmmaker's real talent is in helping us discover "history from the bottom up," enlivening it for people who might not ever think of picking up a multi-volume history of a war, or who don't think they're necessarily interested in jazz, the Shakers, or baseball.

"It's about people," he emphasizes.

"Even in the big series—or especially in the big series—the constituent building block there has been biography. *Civil War* is essentially a series of biographies . . . For World War II, we focused entirely on a bottom-up view of four geographically distributed American towns using the biographies of the people there as a way to tell about the most complicated event in American history.

"And I think it's also about race, I don't like to be very far from that because I do think it's the central question. Afro-American history is at the center of our national existence."

For that reason, race has been a key element in nearly all of Burns' documentaries, from those dealing with jazz and baseball to the Civil War and, of course, Thomas Jefferson.

"When you have our creed being written—the second sentence of the Declaration of Independence—'that all men are created equal,' but he owns more than a hundred human beings and doesn't see the contradiction, then you know that race is at the center of who we are," Burns says.

## Upstairs, Downstairs

As he speaks, a photo portrait showing baseball great Jackie Robinson over his head seems to grow in prominence. It's one of several posters from the filmmaker's PBS documentaries that grace the walls of his offices. Framed promotional posters also adorn the walls of his production studios, which are in a Greek Revival house on a side street in the tiny New Hampshire village of Walpole. Jack Johnson and Billie Holiday along with Mark Twain, Susan B. Anthony, and Elizabeth Cady Stanton look on in each of the rooms, where more than a dozen production assistants, editors, researchers, and interns work simultaneously on Burns's upcoming works.

"There's something incredibly difficult about how we work," says Burns, who spent ten years and more than fifteen million dollars making *America's Parks* and is often involved in the writing, editing, filming, and interviewing processes. "Our job is to make it look effortless."

Along the way, he's won ten Emmy Awards, been nominated for two Oscars, and won a Grammy Award, a Peabody Award, and other recognition. Burns's younger brother, Ric, is an award-winning documentary filmmaker in his own right, with Peabody and Emmy awards to his credit.

Ken Burns travels around the country filming, fundraising, and speaking at colleges and to groups. Then he returns to the tranquility of this town along the Connecticut River. "To be able to come back here is so fantastically restorative. I can come in here at six in the morning, as I did today, work a couple of hours, then go to the editing room where I normally work from eight to five, then come back here to an hour's worth of work, and be that close to my kids." Burns has three daughters, the youngest of whom just turned five.

"That close" is the few hundred feet that separate his business offices and the 180-year-old home Burns moved to in 1979.

This spot next to home is where he and a handful of staffers do desk work on grant proposals, editing scripts, answering e-mails, or having phone conversations on one of the six projects he's currently pushing ahead. This morning, there was also a phone call with a thirteen-year-old Somerville, Massachusetts girl who'd written to him about her school project on a visit with her family to Alaska's Denali National Park.

Before traveling to Boston late in the day for an interview with historian David McCullough on a seven part, fourteen-hour series on the Roosevelts, Burns heads to the editing room in his production studios, where he typically spends the bulk of his days.

Here, in a space dominated by computers, monitors, and editing equipment, he'll sit beside co-producer Paul Barnes and two production assistants. Each is armed with a ten-page notebook transcript of a filmed interview with Theodore Roosevelt scholar Patricia O'Toole. They are watching her image on a large monitor to identify, number, and bracket "selects" that could find a place in the series. The segments will trace the Roosevelts from Theodore to Franklin and Eleanor. Burns says *The Roosevelts: An Intimate History* is "a very interesting psychological drama but also, of course, an outward political history of the first half of the twentieth century."

In Burns's own version of the 1970s PBS series *Upstairs, Downstairs*, editors, technicians, co-producers, and researchers work on various productions in each old bedroom of the sprawling, overcrowded old house with chandeliers overhead, wide-board wooden floors below, and baroque molding on the walls.

One former closet has even been turned into an acoustically modified sound studio with a large microphone for Burns to record the initial "scribe narration"— indicating his preferred pacing—of a documentary's script. His narration will be used to cue visual images, and then it will be dubbed over by a professional narrator.

### Bathtub Gin to Dust Bowl

In one room of the old house, editors are looking over footage of baseball sequences for *The Tenth Inning*, the two-part follow-up to *Baseball*.

"*Baseball* really reflects who we are as an American culture," Burns says. "I thought, after 2004, wouldn't it be great to update the series? Because it continues to be a precise mirror."

The four-hour history of what's taken place since *Baseball* left off, reflecting the changes in which "we've moved away from an African-American narrative to an Hispanic and Asian one and embraced the monetary foolishness that's gotten us into so much trouble and the kind of pharmacological society we've become."

In another room, interns pore over images for a three-part series on Prohibition.

"One's image is always of Model Ts careening around rain-slicked Chicago streets with machine guns blasting," Burns says with a smile. The first episode takes place a hundred years before Prohibition took effect, "when a very admirable idea, temperance—drinking less in a country filled with drunkards—masticated into a single-issue, right-wing lobbying effort that resulted in the Eighteenth Amendment."

The next two *Prohibition* episodes follow "a wonderfully complicated story that reminds you there's nothing new under the sun, that everything we think is unique today—smear campaigns, contested elections, single-issue lobby groups, unfunded mandates, unintended consequences—are part of human dynamics."

A third project, for which an intern is indexing computerized 1930s newspaper clippings, is a two-part history of The Dustbowl—what Burns calls "the greatest manmade ecological catastrophe in American history superimposed on the greatest economic catastrophe in the history of the world."

There's a relaxed feel in the production studios, with some workers walking around in their socks. Many are wearing blue fleece *America's Parks* vests, yet all of them are pushing forward on *Tenth Inning* and then *Prohibition*, with *Dust Bowl* and *The Roosevelts* ramping up behind.

Beyond those projects are others in the offing: a major series on Vietnam timed to coincide with the twentieth anniversary of the fall of Saigon, a documentary on country music, and a film on the 1989 Central Park jogger rape case in which five black and Latino youth were convicted for a crime they didn't commit. Sarah Burns, the filmmaker's daughter, is completing a book based on her Yale thesis on the watershed incident and will be a co-producer of the documentary.

"No matter how hard people try," Burns says, "history always ends up being exclusive. I've struggled really hard to paint, with as a broad a stroke as I can, without sacrificing specificity and honesty. I want these to be honest, complicated portraits that are unafraid of controversy and tragedy, but also are drawn to the things that animate our souls."

And people, by the millions, are truly animated by those stories of people.

"I'm stunned by the variety of people who write to me," Burns says. "It belies the superficial argument that PBS is elitist. I've been stunned by the number of people who write who have been moved to change their feelings to some degree about race. I've been stunned by how impossible it is to go anywhere in the United States and not end up—in an airport, in a small-town, in a diner—in a conversation with somebody that's continuing a conversation they think they've already been having with me.

From his small-town director's perch, where he works to convey the breadth of American history, Burns adds, "It isn't about celebrity. It's about the need to tell me that their great-great-grandfather was in the Civil War, that their grandfather played Triple-A Baseball, that their father served in the Second World War, that their uncle was a jazz musician, that they just visited Denali National Park."

People's eagerness to share that connection with him, Burns says, is "the highest form of compliment."

**Paula Green**

# Our Common Denominator

### June 30, 2014

*Paula Green's work around the world—translating her skills as a therapist to foster peacebuilding—was an unfolding story I pursued numerous times, and she became a friend and neighbor. This account combines elements of Paula's work as founding director of a program at the School for International Training aimed at addressing conflicts globally with her missions in a variety of cultures. In 2017, she began working also to bridge the cultural divide in this country. That Hands Across the Hills effort between folks in western Massachusetts and eastern Kentucky, which I covered extensively, received coverage in the* New York Times *and other media nationally and internationally.*

———

They come from Algeria and Tibet, from Bangladesh and Myanmar, from Kosovo and Palestine. And also come from around the United States.

Each of the students, ages twenty-five to seventy-five, is learning about "conflict transformation" skills they hope to bring back home, in many cases to war-torn, repressive, or fractious societies to shape a peaceful future.

71

Since 1997, this peacebuilding program has gathered teachers, lawyers, and workers for nongovernment organizations and other realms in 125 countries over six continents. On the School for International Training's Brattleboro, Vermont campus, participants in the conflict transformation program meet people from other countries, cultures, and religions, some of which may have been branded the enemy by their own tribes or governments.

And they meet themselves.

"We're trying to build a container for transformation here," says Conflict Transformation Across Cultures Director Paula Green, who founded the CONTACT program in 1996.

Green, who also teaches SIT's master's-level peace and conflict course and was founding director of the Karuna Center for Peacebuilding in Amherst, had been traveling from one global conflict to another to mediate peaceful solutions.

"I found myself telling people in one country what peace efforts were being made in another country," Green says, "so I felt like I was a bird carrying messages of strategies for development of peace and justice. I had a vision of finding a way for people from zones of conflict to speak together, to help inspire people to build solidarity, to find common ground."

This summer, for the first time, there is a participant from the People's Republic of China, plus one from Tibet and a Tibetan refugee living in India. There are also Indians and Pakistanis, and in other years, there have been Israelis with Palestinians as well as participants from different ethnic groups in the former Yugoslavia and in the Caucasus region, all working together.

"They can't meet each other until they get here because they can't cross the borders," Green says of this session's two Indian and four Pakistani participants. "They're together all the time here, and they're loving it."

Abraham Wang, a resident of China's Anhui province who recently graduated from the University of Pennsylvania master's program in teaching English for Speakers of Other Languages, says this has been his first chance to meet Tibetans.

"This affects me enormously," Wang says, "because the government propaganda I have received is all about the amazing work the Chinese government has done for the Tibetan people, how it's played the role of rescuer saving people from slavery, how the international community is unreasonable on this issue . . .

"The opportunity in this program to talk to people from the other side, face to face, is really eye-opening. Certainly it has broadened my perspective. At the end of the day it's about peace, about people living their lives peacefully."

Peace isn't just another word for the participants, who one morning heard a presentation from Kevin Clements of the University of Otago in New Zealand about the Global Peace Index, an annual ranking of the peacefulness of 158 nations according to 23 criteria. They learn how their own countries were ranked in 2012 when Iceland, Denmark, and New Zealand topped the list and Somalia, Afghanistan, and Sudan ranked last with the United States at number 88.

They discuss the underpinnings of most peaceful nations: well-functioning government, sound business environment, equitable resource distribution, low corruption, free information flow, high education levels, acceptance of others' rights, and good neighbor relations.

Their assignment, for which they break into small work groups, is to develop policies and specific strategies for encouraging those characteristics in their home countries.

## A Big Divide

In addition to round-the-clock, informal interactions during their three weeks, participants discuss conditions in their countries as they meet with people from countries in conflict with one another, and share in interreligious conversations.

"That's really a big divide in the world," says Green, with a focus on the core teachings of peacefulness that often are misunderstood or practiced incorrectly.

Discussions may center on women in Islam, on political corruption, on the effects of social media and its censorship by governments. Pointing to public protests in Turkey, Green repeats Turkish Prime Minister Recep Tayyip Erdogan's statement that Twitter is "the worst menace to society."

She comments on how much the rise of social media has contributed to program participants' sense of personal efficacy.

"In 1997 we were barely using computers, and there was almost no Internet, so we were sending out brochures in a way that seems very primitive now. Everything's on Facebook now, so the minute it's posted, they have all these materials to take back with them and use and disseminate.

"It's wonderful for them. They're communicating twenty-four/seven with everybody back home but also with each other."

The Dalai Lama in 2009 honored Green as an "unsung hero of compassion" from the nonprofit Wisdom in Action for her own peacebuilding work.

Green had been a psychotherapist working in Amherst and teaching psychology at Antioch University New England in 1993 when she decided to close her practice, end her teaching career, and take a year's sabbatical in Asia with her husband, Jim Perkins.

She'd been active in the peace movement since the Vietnam era and was a mother with young children while working on her master's degree at New York University at the height of antiwar protests there.

"The world was exploding and I was very engaged against the war. At NYU, I was at the center of the college protests . . . I put my soul into that opposition. Many people went through that, and some people put it aside and went on to other things. For me, it rooted deeply in my soul and became part of my life."

Green later studied Buddhism and in 1974 moved back to New England, where she earned a doctorate in counseling psychology from Boston University and served on the boards of several international peace organizations.

During the sabbatical year, then, Green and Perkins pursued their own spiritual growth as they made their way through India, Nepal, Thailand, and Cambodia. The year solidified Green's resolve to meld her interests in human behavior and peace activism.

"I felt a strong calling to combine the two in something substantive."

She'd seen nonviolence training and conflict resolution as part of organizations she had been associated with. Moved by the extreme poverty, social injustice, and suffering she had witnessed, Green knew it was time to roll up her sleeves to help bring about social change. "It began to feel like this was the work I was being called to do."

Since 1994, she's crisscrossed the globe as founding executive director of Karuna Center, which has since grown to include a host of ongoing programs working with partner groups around the world. She joined SIT's graduate faculty in 1997, teaching courses in conflict transformation and peace building.

Looking at what she created at CONTACT, Green says, "I'm really interested in the transformation of our own attitudes and behaviors as well as the transformation of the unjust institutions that undermine societies, that lock us into certain ways of being, and create the injustices that keep fomenting conflicts.

Some students may arrive wondering how they can help build peaceful solutions. But at CONTACT, she says, "they get inspired to build networks in and beyond their own country to advocate for social change. They get the sense these problems are interconnected and interdependent, and that both causes and solutions lie in great massive change."

## A Blessing

Medard Kakombe, a refugee from the Democratic Republic of Congo now living in Mozambique, cries because his wife and his three children have never met the parents he left behind.

"The first week I spent here," he says, "It was like I was behind a closed door; now it is like someone opened the door. It is a blessing for me, because I am learning from other people who are here. I have come to a point of seeing I'm not alone, learning how other people are facing and managing the conflict they are in."

Pierre-Celestin Bakunda, an emigre from Rwanda now teaching at a French university, says, "I want to find a way to reconcile my people, my compatriots. These two ethnic groups—Hutus and Tutsis—have been fighting for power for ages.

"I blame both of them. The legacy of this hate is not good for our future generations. We should sit around the negotiation table so we can find a solution, so we can follow the example of South Africa and Northern Ireland."

Bakunda, who lost eighteen family members in Rwandan fighting that intensified just before he left in 1995, adds, "There are so many, many difficulties, because a group has held power and they don't want to share power . . . Economically, people are so marginalized and poor. We want a fair state where people can co-exist peacefully and encourage this kind of democracy."

Another Rwandan, Jean-Luc Dushime, who now works as a photographer, writer and storyteller in Vermont, recalls walking for six months to escape genocide in his country. He went to the Democratic Republic of Congo, where he lived for seven years before arriving here in 2004.

"That was when all the pain and suffering hit, when I was in a peaceful place, when I had enough time to reflect on what happened to me. I became an artist to express my frustration and my hopes. Then I realized how much I've changed in terms of identity."

Dushime, who lost many family members and childhood friends in Rwanda as well as friends in the Congo because of the civil war there, returned to his native country this spring for the first time in eighteen years.

"I went back home as a new person, and it was an interesting perspective, meeting a new country. That's when I realized I needed more tools to find solutions in a peaceful way, because I am sick of war. I feel I really want to be part of a solution. How do we share our country and move forward? My biggest goal is to bring Hutus and Tutsis to the table and help them listen to each other, because we've suffered so much that we dismiss each other's pain."

Lamia Lahrech, one of five Algerian women participating in CONTACT, says the diverse group is learning nonviolent ways to improve healthcare, education, economic, and social systems in their countries while discovering ways to begin working together.

"For me," says the Algerian dentist, "it's just trying to find a common humanity in all of us . . . and stop thinking about the differences."

## Depicting the Cycle

"Two forces are in constant battle inside each of us, and in the world," a grandfather tells his young grandson: "Good and Evil."

"But which will win?" asks the boy.

"The one we feed."

Rwandan author and lecturer Joseph Sebarenzi shares this story with more than fifty-five CONTACT participants from twenty-five countries completing the first of three weeks of the retreat.

"Can there be true reconciliation without justice?" the students ask, considering how stereotypes of 'the other' are manipulated by politicians, the media, and other forces in society.

Even in the days just before renewed violence exploded between Shiite and Sunni factions in Iraq, participants are looking at ongoing human-rights struggles and oppressive regimes in nations some of us have known little about.

Sebarenzi's talk precedes a particularly heart-wrenching CONTACT session in which the cycle-of-violence chart, discussed a couple of hours earlier, is replicated on the carpet of our large meeting room.

The participants, myself included, have spent time thinking about our own hidden prejudices and revealing them to one another. Now we're asked to place our bodies on a marked spot on the floor of a cycle depicting the inner conflicts that we're all feeling: fear, self-blame, anger, sadness, memorializing, teaching tolerance, desire for revenge.

Each of the Rwandan, Liberian, Tibetan, South Sudanese, Indian, Burmese, and other students has staked out positions near signs marking the cycle stages.

Like some of the other Americans in the group—including an ex-marine confronting his combat attitudes and actions—I look around the room, considering where I belong.

I think of the films we've just seen about horrendous carnage in Bosnia, in Nigeria and Liberia, nations where religious and ethnic groups had lived peacefully for centuries before turning violent.

I look at the faces around the room, at black and brown and yellow and white faces of friends whose eyes we've searched deeply for a few days. I consider news accounts of recent honor killings, kidnappings and attacks.

I sit at *mourning/grief*.

The knot in my own stomach is tied, too, with sadness about what our own country is seeing: growing economic injustice, a swelling minority prison population, and a breakdown of democratic institutions fed by increasing political and social polarization. Slowly, each of us is asked to explain the moment's anger, grief, fear, confusion.

"I ask myself, 'Why did it happen?'" says a Rwandan woman seated on the floor near *suppression of grief*. Like many in the program, she works for a nonprofit organization aimed at reconciling her nation's ethnic divide.

A man from one battle-worn African country seated near *anger/ why me?* says, "Since I was born, I can never be happy . . . sometimes I just cry because of the suffering. Without peace, nothing will be better in my country."

I place my arm around him to offer comfort.

A Tibetan refugee explains his inner conflict between forgiveness and longing for his homeland to be free. A young Yemeni shares his frustration at watching the Arab Spring melt away. Several women break down in anguish as they reveal having been raped or witnessing their daughters being sexually violated by militia groups.

The marine, seated at *rehumanizing the enemy*, tells us that after September 11, "I hated Muslims. I didn't even see them as humans. I didn't look on terrorists as people. I looked on them as targets."

When it comes time to act on an order to kill a suspected Somali terrorist enjoying a meal with his wife and two young sons, "We laughed because it was so easy. I'd joined thinking if I could kill enough terrorists, the war would be over. I created three more," he says, holding back tears.

A long, profound silence fills the room.

We focus on how the cycle of violence plays out again and again between ethnic groups that most of us can hardly differentiate, between religions or tribes or other divisions that barely make sense.

The violence erupting between sects or tribes is never truly about those apparent differences, Green says repeatedly. Instead, it's incited by leaders corrupted by their own power. The underlying cause of violent conflicts—more prone to restart where there's been a history of violence—is injustice.

## Another Cycle

CONTACT's founding director has seen the cycle play out again and again—everywhere.

"Many of the wars we're seeing now have roots in history that have never been healed, so it repeats itself in another cycle," she laments. "It may take another generation, but it does."

And then, as much of a surprise to her as anybody, soon after retiring from leadership of CONTACT and the Karuna Center in 2016, Green spearheaded an attempt by her town of Leverett to launch a bridge-building effort, dubbed Hands Across the Hills, with residents of Letcher County, Kentucky. The project, a response to the 2016 election, has tried to help their very different communities search for commonalities at a frightening time of increasing political polarization in this country.

Although it's a painstaking effort requiring perseverance and patience, Green says, building those bridges "is giving people hope in a pretty hopeless time, when a lot of people are feeling pretty disempowered about the political situation. Changing the cultural behavior going on right now is something that seems impossible until you've tried it."

Ben Fink, a community organizer in Letcher County, says, "This is a long game ... If we're going to make the world different, where we recognize that we've been divided, where we set out to defeat the culture wars, where these sides no longer exist, the work has got to be done in a whole lot of different ways, where we don't see each other as enemies."

Green adds, "This is about finding common ground and trying to dispel the stereotypes and demonization of each other, because that threatens our country and our democracy. "We talk about politics, we talk about religion, we talk about class. We're just not here to convert each other, we're here to understand each other." We're not here to change each other; we're here to learn from each other and accept the differences and acting on the commonalities."

*Portions of this story were published in 2004, 2013, and 2018.*

Robert J. Lurtsema

# Waking up with Lurtsema

## November 6, 1980

*This story about radio's syndicated classical music host Robert J. Lurtsema, of whom I had been a fan, was written as a magazine piece. In the Saturday morning interview during his broadcast in WGBH studios in Boston, I accidentally invoked the Lurtsema's wrath by engaging him in a conversation between musical selections that caused him to miss his cue when a recording ended. He uttered a mild profanity and apologized to his radio audience, confiding, "This is why I swore I'd never give interviews while I'm on the air!"*

He's been called "offbeat . . . quirky . . . the most creative newscaster in America."

But Robert J. Lurtsema, the inimitable host of National Public Radio's *Morning Pro Musica*, is most aptly described by the simple birdsong that opens his seven-day-a-week classical music program.

Listening to Lurtsema is sipping a cup of café au lait.

His baritone voice almost grumbles smoothly, yet it's hardly the silver-throated clarity that oozes from some easy-listening announcers.

Lurtsema himself is far less smooth, breaking all canons of radio announcing.

He shrugs off one writer's labeling him "a culture cult figure," preferring what another has dubbed "the cult of calm."

Lurtsema seems so languid, so low-key that, in the words of one writer, he "seems to be swaying on the edge of a coma."

But at 7 AM, when Lurtsema begins his five-hour broadcast from WGBH in Boston, he sounds more like a bathrobed, overnight houseguest you've stumbled upon in your hallway, someone saluting with a groggy "good morning" on the way to the bathroom before breakfast.

Lurtsema, 48, is short, stocky, and quite bald with wispy, bushy white sideburns.

A little ornery, a bit sarcastic, the soft-spoken impressario of the classical airwaves perches on his orange swivel throne in cramped Studio 4 just south of the Charles River in Boston.

Sporting black sandals with black socks, black pants, and a blue shirt, the sultan chainsmokes and sips coffee from an oversized black pottery mug with fern imprints.

But he is busy engineering his own program with recordings selected from the station's thirty-five-thousand-volume record library, and keeping logs of what he airs.

Lurtsema is dedicated to his music and his loyal listeners, and if management or media attention get in the way, he becomes a bit feisty.

"If I seem somewhat cynical, I am," he admits.

Robert J., as devotees refer to him, grumbles about lingering media attention to a three-month battle in which Lurtsema lovers lobbied to have the network reinstate his unique newscasts.

A network study, Lurtsema explains, "says everybody instantly upon waking wants to know the grim details of every story that's happening everywhere."

He disagrees, and loyal fans swamped the station with three thousand letters backing Lurtsema's uniquely anticlimactic newscasts instead of those of a more professional sounding newscaster. Three months after his newscasts were taken off the air, the station threw in the towel.

"When listeners wake up," says Lurtsema, "they want to know the world is still here. The news has to be there, but the music is paramount.

"Obviously if a listener is looking for the latest coverage of fires, muggings, rapes, stabbings, he's looking to the wrong source, because I virtually eliminate it," says Lurtsema. Sometimes, in fact, Lurtsema skips the news altogether because he believes nothing that day is newsworthy.

"If the show has a calming influence," he reflects, "that's good."

Unlike most well-prepared announcers, Lurtsema takes time for dramatic lulls and pensiveness, exhaling slowly and repeatedly pausing long enough to make you wonder whether he has indeed gone into a coma.

"Sometimes I sound to people as if I'm making the news up as I go along," says Lurtsema, who wakes at 5:30, drives in from nearby Wellesley by 6:30, makes a pot of coffee, and quickly scans the night's newswire copy, *The Times*, *The Globe*, *The Herald*, and *The Wall Street Journal*.

"Sometimes I read stories exactly as they come off the wire, they're the way I would have written them myself. Sometimes I put them in my own words. An exact word comes up, and I can't think of it. How long can you sit there and wait for the word to come up without substituting a weaker word?"

Regular listeners have learned the virtue of patience. He who hesitates is worth it.

"I'm not afraid of dead air," Lurtsema has been quoted as saying. "When I pause, I'm visualizing my audience, the person I'm speaking to. I always imagine I'm speaking to someone in particular."

But, as Lurtsema stresses, *Morning Pro Musica* is "first and foremost a program of music . . . a program about music and the people who make the music."

There are live interviews, live performances, and often tributes to specific composers and performers.

Lurtsema wants his program not only to enlighten and entertain listeners who know about concert music but also those who don't.

He often combines traditional, folk, and popular music from foreign countries, set around their national holidays.

"Radio has always been something I could fall back on when I needed money," says Lurtsema, who was born and raised in the Boston area. "It was always one way to pay the milk bills."

Lurtsema, who's held an array of jobs ranging from lumberjack to encyclopedia salesman, from trapeze artist to construction worker, also worked for several years on Boston's commercial classical station WCRB and then for a New York City advertising agency and radio outlet. He even managed a national chain of discotheques for teenagers. Back in Boston, he was absorbed in painting fulltime in 1971 when he telephoned WGBH one weekend to correct something he'd heard on the air.

The announcer had been taped, but the engineer tipped him off that a weekend announcing job was available.

Four months after taking the job, Lurtsema was asked to work weekdays instead. He protested, believing the program needed the continuity of one person planning and announcing seven days a week.

He's been on ever since.

Lurtsema does a skeleton outline of his programs a year in advance, then fleshes it out three months before it goes on the air.

In July of 1980, *Morning Pro Musica,* which had been carried over a half dozen public radio stations in New York and New England, went nationwide. But the syndication leaves Robert J. cold.

Lurtsema, who says disgustedly that he has no idea how many stations air the program, feels a strong need to relate to the audience—something nationwide syndication impedes, he says. Some estimates have put Lurtesma's following at 120 radio stations with as many as half a million listeners, mostly across New England and upstate New York.

One reason is that West Coast listeners pick up only the last three hours of the program, at 6 AM their time.

"I plan the program in a chronological way. I'm saving twentieth-century compositions for the last hour when the listeners are more awake. For many people, that hour is the first thing they're going to hear. If they have something that's modern, complex, dissonant, that's wrong. But I just keep doing what I have to. If they want to take the program, fine."

At 11:39, Lurtsema looks at the digital clock in front of him and reflects on his future in radio.

"There are twenty-one minutes I'm sure of. Beyond that, I'm not."

If he left the program, as he has threatened on occasion to do, "I would not go back to work in radio. There are too many things that are less frustrating and that certainly are more financially rewarding." Lurtsema, who studied meteorology and later media and journalism at Boston University, sleeps only four or five hours a night.

"That leaves me time to squeeze in more activities than most people get involved with," he explains. "There's never been any time in my life when I just did one thing. Nothing held my interest sufficiently.

"I never had a formal course in music until I started at the New England Conservatory. I got to the point where I realized there were a great many things I only had a sketchy knowledge of—or none at all.

He reminisces fondly about his days in theatre—which he would like to do more—and less romantically about his sculpting.

There are spin-off projects from radio: a book of interviews with performers and composers, a recording of Christmas and Chanukkah stories, a record on loons.

He studies composition at New England Conservatory and wants to do more musical composition. He also paints—mostly dawnscapes.

"Dawn is something I've become intimately familiar with," he says.

Yet Lurtsema's best-known dawnscape is *Morning Pro Musica* itself.

"Every day there is that blank canvas on which to paint a five-hour program. Some days, there's a lot of wasted paint. Some days, it's a masterpiece. The negative side is that radio is an ephemeral medium," he muses.

"The program goes on, it goes off. It's not like you know when you finish a painting, that it's a good work, it has some merit, it has some lasting value."

What does endure are the birds, which softly herald the program's opening each morning, chirping a few minutes alone and then in the background as a prelude to the theme music that varies by day of the week, from Respighi's "Ancient Airs and Dances" to the adagio from Bach's Concerto for two Harpsichords or Handel's "Arrival of the Queen of Sheba."

And then arrives the sonorous voice of Lurtsema himself with a somewhat groggy, "Good morning."

Lurtsema had heard a chickadee as he was leaving for work one day and decided to open the program with the chirping. It grew day-by-day and has become a ritual for thousands of Lurtsemaphiles.

The culmination occurred last year, when Lurtsema hung

microphones in the trees during live broadcasts from Tanglewood summer music festival in the Berkshires.

And it all came home to roost recently in a little girl's question to Lurtsema: "How do you get the birds to stop?" asked the girl, who'd imagined a row of birds singing in what is Studio 4.

"I have very obedient birds," he replied.

*Robert J. Lurtsema died in June 2000*

photo by Rami Efal

**meditation retreat at Auschwitz**
# In Touch with Sorrow
### December 12, 2010

*Having grown up at a time when most Holocaust survivors could not even begin to talk about the trauma they'd experienced not so many years before, I was inspired hearing about friends who'd chosen to participate in interfaith pilgrimages to Nazi death camps to "bear witness" to what had taken place there decades earlier, opening their hearts to find a deeper, universal meaning about their own humanity and inhumanity. I know the following will be a difficult story for some readers to accept, and it was challenging to write from a distance. But I felt it important to share.*

———

The very name of this place chills the blood: Auschwitz.

Especially in November, when the cold wind blows through the stark, open landscape, across the mud, and through the barracks where hundreds of thousands awaited extermination, Auschwitz seems like the most unimaginably awful place for an annual pilgrimage for self-reflection.

And yet, organizers and some participants of the five-day retreat to the Nazi death camp—like the one the Montague-based Zen Peacemakers ran last month—say the Polish landmark is an almost "sacred" place with potential to bring inner peace, even an "aliveness."

The site of the extermination camp, to which 1.3 million human beings were deported from 1940 to 1945—and where 1.1 million of them were murdered—Auschwitz today is a museum near the Polish village of Oswiecim.

It receives more than a million visitors a year. The 52-acre Auschwitz camp and the neighboring 425-acre Birkenau site a couple of miles away were the largest of the 10 Nazi death camps. The Nazis ran hundreds of smaller prison, labor, and detention camps in Germany and occupied countries.

Most of the visitors, who arrive in groups to examine the forty-six buildings, wear on their faces a stark look that says, "This is horrible! Get me out of here," reflects Eve Marko, a meditation teacher and one of the leaders of the Buddhist order's annual Bearing Witness retreats at Auschwitz.

"Everybody else is coming and going," she says. "But if you stay, you find something else: It's a place of enormous energy. It's very sacred."

That spiritual energy, which other participants also describe, "is just there, to be felt and experienced—and worked with. It makes you question everything. It inspires you. It rededicates you. It totally changed my life," says Marko, who is Jewish.

A peaceful, beautiful setting is more typically imagined as the ideal meditation place.

But during the Buddhist order's retreats at Auschwitz—like those it conducts on the streets of New York, Boston, and cities around the world—the purpose of meditation "is to make you as alive as possible," Marko says.

"When people are at Auschwitz, they do discover that quality of aliveness in a very strong way."

The retreats grew out of a 1994 convocation organized by area peace activist Paula Green involving monks from the Leverett Peace Pagoda on a trek to Hiroshima.

At Auschwitz, Zen Peacemakers founder Bernie Glassman meditated on the death camp itself and realized, "There are amazing things that happen in this place."

Glassman, who felt the presence of ghosts inhabiting Auschwitz, wrote in his 1998 book *Bearing Witness* that the camps were dedicated to annihilating all difference: wiping out entire communities of Jews, Gypsies, homosexuals, leftists, the mentally ill, retarded, physically disabled, and other groups the Nazis labeled as undesirables.

The retreats, then, which Glassman and Marko began in 1996, were designed to embrace as many countries, cultures, and religions as possible.

"Auschwitz was the Nazis' solution to diversity—just to destroy it completely," says Marko. "We recreate that. We bring so many different people from different countries. And they do get on each other's nerves, because that's what happens."

Retreat organizer Ginni Stern adds, "We celebrate diversity. I share a meal with somebody I'd probably not share a meal with or sit and realize, 'Oh. I can sit with this German woman whose father was a Nazi? And could maybe even share a room with her and share stories in the dark at night? Or share toothpaste?'

"There's difference everywhere if you look for it. We could celebrate it. Or be frightened by it. Or see it as 'other' that needs to be changed or be different. Or annihilated."

Last month's retreat, with eighty participants from Israel, Poland, Germany, Italy, Switzerland, and the United States, featured the first young people's contingent with sixteen participants ages sixteen to twenty-four.

Over the years, the retreats have drawn participants from Latin America, Rwanda, Sierra Leone, Ireland, Bosnia, and elsewhere. Among the religious leaders have been priests, rabbis, Buddhist monks, imams, Wiccans, and American Indian medicine men.

"It's a huge 'heart' that everybody feels here, from each other, from the staff," says Marko. "But I think it's all about the place. We say that the place is the leader here."

### Emotionally Exhausted

The barbed wire perimeter around the desolate abandoned death camp seems endless as the camera travels its length, then turns a corner and pans every inch of its width in Cristof Wolf's award-winning 2008 documentary, *In Spite of Darkness*.

The film, exploring *A Spiritual Encounter with Auschwitz,* records a 2006 Bearing Witness retreat through the eyes of four of its fifty participants. Stern was among them.

There are waves of overwhelming shock, of endless tears, of profound compassion.

And much more. Many other groups of visitors wince their way through a tour of the men's and women's barracks, the crematorium, the ash pit.

Yet the Zen-inspired pilgrims linger for five days, wandering off to intimately encounter the ghosts in the shadows of that place where the haunting cries and timeless stench in the cold air seem palpable seven decades after the murderous reign of terror.

"I thought I was going to Auschwitz, but by opening my heart, I think I let Auschwitz come to me," says John Richardson, a 2006 participant from New Mexico, who admits to being "emotionally exhausted" and, at one point, filled with anger at the Holocaust's perpetrators.

"There was anger at the inhumanity. But I wanted to go deeper. I wanted to get in touch with the sorrow."

Christiane Wenzl, a Swiss woman struggling to come to terms with her grandfather's Nazi past, tells the film's interviewer, "I felt my soul was called to Auschwitz. It's beyond words."

There, through reflection, she learns that the perpetrator/victim dichotomy is not absolute. That raised deeper questions about herself: "When do I go over limits and when do I hurt somebody or when do I judge? Where is this limit when I'm not at peace with myself or others?"

Israeli Rabbi Ohad Ezrahi leads interfaith kaddish services, a mourning sanctification prayer, with participants in the women's barracks and at the outdoor "killing wall." In the film, he acknowledges, "Since we are not different, I could be a Nazi. I have a little Nazi in me. That's not easy to recognize or say. The potential of dehumanizing 'the other' is there."

He returned to Israel after one retreat as Israel was being closed off to Palestinians and found there a refusal among many "to acknowledge the suffering on the other side. They jump to another subject: 'Stop! I'll have mercy on them and not be able to see them as the enemy.'"

Ezrahi plays guitar to accompany a group singing lullabies in the children's barracks as a way to comfort souls of the terrified and murdered young victims. He also leads a controversial ceremony in an Auschwitz watchtower in remembrance of the sentries who would shoot anyone they took to be trying to escape.

"I collapse after this ceremony," he says. "It just squeezes me."

The rabbi, who admits that no one in his family experienced the horrors of the Holocaust firsthand, rejects the way that some Jewish groups have claimed that history as theirs alone.

"Auschwitz is part of the history of humankind. I am tied to this place in some mysterious way. I leave with this holding of life and death and a commitment to serve God through both."

## Very Thorny Questions

Auschwitz has a way of grating on people's nerves.

Some participants, anxious about the whole experience, describe how jarring it can be from the moment they board the plane to Poland and hear the German language from crew members.

A lot of hot buttons for people are pushed in that emotional environment: Jews, Arabs, Germans, Poles.

Planning discussions, says Marko, probed the potential for impossibly charged realities. "Sending young people to different religious services and what it's like for Jews to hear 'Allah' at a place like Auschwitz? It really is mind-blowing. It really is tough for people. It's tough for people."

In large evening gatherings, retreat members share openly and emotionally the horrors they come face to face with each day—the selection yard where the Nazis separated women from men and from children, deciding who was strong enough to go into forced labor and who would be immediately murdered; the crematorium; the killing wall where prisoners were executed before the building of gas chambers.

Raw emotions fly.

Marko recalls, "We've had people who were upset: 'How could you say this?' 'How could they feel that way?' 'Why do you let those people in the retreat?' And then there are just people with their own reactions, and they always offend somebody.

"We've had people say, 'You let that person speak. I'm out of here.'" When a German staff member suggested one year that a ritual to memorialize the names of those murdered at Auschwitz be extended to include the names of guards, it almost tore apart the whole retreat. One rabbi says, 'If you're going to do that, I'm never coming back here, I'm never bringing any of my students back here.'"

One woman, Marko recalls, came to Auschwitz angry and left furious.

"She left saying, 'You know how I'm feeling? I wish I had six million bullets to kill Germans with!'"

Planning last month's retreat with its first dedicated cohort of young people, organizers realized the political realities of Jewish and Palestinian participants as well as Germans and Poles, might produce yet another powder keg.

"These are very tricky questions we're going to be dealing with, how to hold a big container where people can express themselves . . . because it's bound to offend people," says Marko. "We can't tell people to muzzle themselves." Ultimately, the Israelis refused to allow visas for the Palestinian students to leave the country. Arab Israeli youth, however, did attend.

Even for Jewish students from Israel—let alone Arabs—taking part in a retreat like those organized by Zen Peacemakers is extremely controversial.

"For the Arabs, there's enormous pressure on them not to go there, not to acknowledge any Jewish suffering," Marko explains. "And even from the Israeli Jewish point of view, you go to Auschwitz as part of the high school groups that are very Zionistic. You walk in with Israeli flags or with the March of the Living. But you do not go as part of a multinational thing. 'This is our place, nobody else's place.' The very fact they're doing that is really politically incorrect."

When past retreats gathered to meditate beside the railroad tracks at the selection yard, Bearing Witness coordinator Stern watched groups of students from Israel, from Germany, and from Poland "walk by each other—and they don't even look at each other. It really disturbed me. How could the Israelis, in particular, leave Auschwitz without growing hate, without increased anger at the Poles and the Germans?"

Then an Israeli teacher offered to find grant money to bring a small group of Jewish and Arab teens to the camp before they reach the age of military conscription and begin confronting each other at checkpoints and conflicts.

For Stern, who has long wanted to bring teens together at Auschwitz, "It was just a dream come true."

If the point of meditation is to drop back to a state of "not knowing," where there is no "other" so we can actually "bear witness" to a deeper reality, then Marko says she doesn't worry about the conflicts that arise when participants speak their truths at Auschwitz.

"There's something so true and raw about it, you can't lie. My trust is of the place," Marko says. "They hear each other, and they bear witness to their own reactions . . . except in this retreat, it leads in a whole different direction than what happened there seventy years ago. It comes out of exactly the fact that there are all these different people: they dress different, they look different, they talk different languages, and there's an enormous intuitive sense of oneness out of it."

## Those Personal Truths

When Stern pushed into the crematorium's ash pit a stone she'd brought to memorialize family members who had been murdered, her hand came out coated in mud flaked with human bone fragments.

"My inclination was to wipe it off. But I didn't want to treat it like garbage. The dirt there is very, very powerful."

Yet the awakenings during the five-day retreats aren't just to the atrocities that happened there, organizers say.

"Everybody finds themselves there," says Marko. "But sometimes what they find has nothing to do with genocide, per se. Maybe what they find is lot of suffering they had as children at the hands of a father or a mother."

Though they might apologize to the group for bringing up an uncovered personal tragedy that seems to pale compared to the Nazi atrocities, the self-reflections that people confront are every bit as real as the Holocaust itself.

Visitors to the death camp's barracks come face to face with the ghosts of the victims. They wonder, "Who passed through here? What if it had been me? My wife or husband? My child?"

Those who spend enough time reflecting at Auschwitz find themselves in a place "tailor made for you to encounter the darkest parts of yourself," Marko says.

Just before Karen Werner of Montague took part in last year's retreat, she met with her parents in Krakow, visiting the area to see where her grandmother had been from. Her mother, whose family had fled Vienna before the Holocaust, was upset that Werner was going on to Auschwitz and gave her a pink scarf to "celebrate life" there.

"What was huge for me was bearing witness to my mom's inability to deal with that place, to hold the grief and the aliveness," Werner recalls. She left her parents and arrived at the death camp terrified by the dirt and the air—"about touching the death there."

By the end of the retreat, she intentionally lay down in the dirt—with the scarf. Then she danced in line at a "truly ecstatic" Shabbat dinner in the Polish village and left Auschwitz able to reconcile her feelings toward her mother. "I forgave her, in a way, for her inability to grieve."

For Stern, who grew up with an abusive father who was a Holocaust survivor, each year's retreat holds a new discovery.

"I feel a shift about holding compassion for him," she says. And after rejecting for years the notion she might have "a Nazi within," Stern discovered that she had cut herself off from co-workers and family who have upset her.

"I don't do that anymore. I feel I really want to challenge that in myself. It's been an exploration of who do I perceive as 'the other?' I've become more courageous in having a dialogue with people about their war experiences or the ripple effect of those experiences."

One German participant at an Auschwitz retreat, Bettina Kaut, who'd kept to herself for the first four days, revealed at the end the secret that was silently eating at her. Her grandfather had been the mayor of a small town, Goch, near the Dutch border. When the Nazis came to Goch demanding to know which were the Jewish homes, her grandfather turned their names over as ordered. All of the Jews were taken away.

"She says, 'This is my story. And I love my grandfather. And now I have to deal with this,'" Marko recalls. Kaut returned to the retreat two years later. "It was like she was another person. She came to me and was just beaming and full of life."

The German woman spent the two years researching what had happened to the Jews of Goch. All had been killed but one. Kaut tracked down that survivor's son in Israel. She then traveled to Jerusalem to meet him to tell him who she was and to hear who he was.

Kaut had a memorial erected in the village and wrote an account of her search.

"She told us what she had done," remembers Marko. "It's like she had gotten her life back. In a place like Auschwitz."

**Johnny Jump Ups**

# "We Dance Up the Sun!"

### April 30, 2014

*My first encounter with morris dancing in 1978 seemed like a hallucinogenic experience, as we stumbled on literally hundreds of dancers assembled for the annual Marlboro Morris Ale, all dressed in white, wearing bells, and clanking sticks as they leaped and moved in graceful rhythmic formation around the campus of Marlboro College.*

*I briefly danced on a morris team a few years later before settling into the simple enjoyment of watching morris teams celebrate the arrival of spring each year around the region, especially at Montague's May Day festivities on the town common. It was watching the youngest dancers enthusiastically carry on this ancient tradition that captured my imagination and drew me to write this story.*

———

At the tippy top of the morning on May Day, six pint-sized dancers, dressed in dashing blue vests and white shirts and pants with jingle bells strapped to their calves, greeted the dawn bounding to the song "Shepherd's Hay" on the Shutesbury Common.

95

It was still dark and cold when the Johnny Jump Ups arrived, their bells shaking off their sleepiness, for the annual ritual. But it was the youthful dancing of those morris dancers—their leaping, their skipping and waving of hankies along with the dancing of groups like the Morning Glories—that seemed to awaken the sun and beckon the spring.

Those ancient pagan dances might just strike new eyes as less than completely serious, especially done by tots. And that's OK. Morris dancing is an ancient ritual about lightening up, no matter how it's done.

After the wearisome winter we've just been through, just watching the Johnny Jump Ups and teams like them can stir a needed sigh of relief.

"I feel really happy," says Libby Hayes of Shutesbury, 6, in anticipation of dancing today as part of her second season with the Jump Ups. "It's usually pretty cold on May Day, but I'm pretty excited, like I'm jumping around inside."

No wonder her favorite dance is "Shooting." When you watch the dancers bounding as high as they can into the air, it dawns on you why the season is called spring.

In all the festivities that abound on May Day weekend with annual Maypole celebrations on the Montague Common and the northern Amherst village of Cushman, the gaggle of raucous adult morris enthusiasts may garner most of the attention.

But young teams like the Jump Ups and others taking to the Shutesbury Common and then on a tour of area schools—Greenfield Center School, Gill, Leverett—are the best indication that morris dancing, an Old England tradition that had reawakened in New England in the 1970s, may have actually rooted.

"It's really nice to pass it on," says Andrea Rogers of Shutesbury, who teaches that troupe of beginning morris dancers from Greenfield, Montague, and other area towns. She and her husband, Geoff, started the team in 2002 when their son Angus was in second grade, drawing largely on kids involved in the annual Welcome Yule pageant at The Shea Theater in Turners Falls.

"He had been following us in morris tours when he was in utero," says Rogers, who joined her first team, Swarth Morris, in 1979 in

Pennsylvania and dances on the Amherst-based Wake Robin team. She had also danced with Bells of the North in Minneapolis, Millstone River at Princeton, and Ha'Penny in Cambridge before moving to the area in 1986.

Geoff, who plays concertina for the Jump Ups, began dancing in 1981 on Juggler Meadow. Angus, who danced with Jump Ups until he was in seventh grade, is nineteen and on Juggler Meadow, even though he's a college student in Maine. His fourteen-year-old sister, Fiona, is an eighth-grader who graduated from the Jump Ups to the teen team And Sometimes Y Manx Morris Sword, which raised money to travel last year to Britain's Isle of Man to perform the rare Manx morris dances there.

Cedar Skinder of Greenfield was only five when she started dancing as a Jump Up last year. "I feel good when I'm dancing because I'm with my family on morris teams. Both Mama and Papa dance," she says.

As shivering as the pre-dawn preparations will be for the Morning Glories and other teams on the Shutesbury Common, says seven-year-old Solena Davidson-Carroll of Montague, the dancers warm up with dances like Three Musketeers, one of her favorites. And although it's only her second year dancing, she remembers that at the Montague Town Common celebration, "it gets really hot dancing if it's a hot day, because we have long shirts and all."

## Awakening a Tradition

Morris dancing dates back to at least the fifteenth century and was originally called moryssh from the French morisque, or Moorish. It had a revival around 1900 thanks to the pioneering work of British folklorist Cecil Sharp, who formed the English Folk Dance Society and published two collections of morris dances in 1905 and 1907. It was in the late 1960s and 1970s that it came alive in this country with the help of Roger Cartwright, often called the Johnny Appleseed of morris in this country.

Cartwright helped form the Village Morris Men in New York City and led a tour of England in 1973. That Pinewoods New Englanders tour spawned creation of several other US morris teams, including New Cambridge Morris Men, which first danced out in 1974 and, soon after, the Marlboro Morris Men in Vermont and a short-lived Berkshire Morris Men in Greenfield in 1978. Cartwright lived in Shutesbury before his death in 2011.

Rogers says many of the morris teams that bound and abound today—Massachusetts has more teams, thirty, than any other state—can be traced back to dancers inspired by Village Morris Men or New Cambridge Morris Men.

"They were all taught by Roger or one generation down," she says. "There's that cohort of people in college or grad school in the seventies who are in our fifties and sixties, so there are lots of morris dancers in that age range. But then there's a lost generation of people in their thirties, who didn't get recruited a lot. And now there are a lot of kids dancing."

## Garlands and Girly-Girls

While it's not precisely morris, the garland dances performed by Morning Glory Girls' Garland are closely related, with girls in white skirts and blouses dancing on the common bearing flower-bedecked half-hoops and jingle bells.

"We're the girly-girls, the pretty ones. We balance the rougher stuff," says leader Laura Wildman-Hanlon of Montague, who started the team in 2011 after being part of all-women Hart's Brook Garland for fifteen years and hearing team members' daughters say, "That looks like fun!"

The hoop dances, which echo the lilting though rough-and-tumble morris steps with what almost seems like skipping, have been traced back to the start of the Industrial Revolution in mill towns of northern England, says Wildman-Hanlon, who believes they may actually be much older than that.

"This was a way to give the women who worked in the factories dancing as a form of exercise," she adds. It doesn't present the same "up-your-nose" attitude toward the gentry that men's morris dancing did. Yet "It's a beautiful style dance," she says, especially when it was brought to the verdant countryside in England, just as it is in rural New England.

Wildman-Hanlon, who admits, "It's a dying tradition," hoped to launch a first-ever all-garland ale, or gathering of dancers, locally to draw the five or six teams from around this country, "to get the garland style out there and stir more interest, before it disappears."

The especially feminine dance form, in frilly costume with colorful waist ribbons, may not be especially popular in a gender-role-defying age when women vie with men on stick-clashing morris teams.

The Morning Glories number just four or five, contrasted with as many as twenty-one in some years, says Wildman-Hanlon. Team members' ages range from seven to twelve when, according to another tradition, interests tend to change and "they become very self-conscious," she says, pointing to a pair of alumnae gabbing in the corner of the Whately Elementary School gym during a recent, pre-season practice.

"I hope that with the girls team, if we get them interested, they'll remember and come back, saying, 'I want to do that again' on an adult team like Hart's Brook," says Wildman-Hanlon, who's also a member of another family morris team, Stick'N the Mist. That team also practices at Whately on Sundays along with the girls' and women's garland teams.

"It's fun," says sixteen-year-old member Orlando Wildman-Hanlon, son of team members Laura Wildman-Hanlon and her husband. In between dances at the Whately gym rehearsal, Orlando shoots baskets in the Whately gym. "We dance a lot of cheerful dances. There's a lot of jumping," adds the former Johnny Jump Up, getting in a dribble or two between shots and commenting about what the morris feels like from inside. "Skipping . . . We use sticks often . . . I get a little nervous when we're dancing out in public. Once we're doing it, it's fun."

Stick 'N the Mist's costume or kit features rags of black, grays, or blues with ribbons and sneakers, black vests, knickers, and fedoras. Standing in a set of four, members strike each other's wooden batons across each person in the set in turn— first low, then high—before turning and doing the same with the corners dancers beside them and then swinging each other, arm in arm, as in a square dance or a contradance, in a boisterous, energetic border morris tradition.

Fourteen-year-old member Emily Menard of Greenfield, who joined the mixed team of adults and kids from Montague, Greenfield, Deerfield, and Cummington, says she's drawn to morris because it connects her with her family's English heritage.

"I'm really into the music," provided by fiddle played by Shelby Howland of Buckland and the button accordion of team leader Peggy Ezell of Whately. "What I like is connecting with my ancestors."

Menard, an eighth grader at Frontier Regional School in Deerfield, joined the Morning Glories in 2011 after she saw a flier. "My friends and I thought it would be fun: we get to dress up in skirts and flowers. That garland feels a lot more graceful. This morris feels a lot . . . " She flexes her bicep with a laugh and a stomp of her foot . . . "manlier."

Although preseason practicing of dances like "Belligerent Blue Jay," "Clockwork," and "Old Bones" was a fun way to knock off any lingering winter blahs, and warming up at last weekend's New England Folk Arts Festival was a thrill, stepping out for May Day is simply glorious.

"It's really, really great," Menard says. "It makes me feel happy. Having an audience adds to the fun." On the Shutesbury Common, "We dance up the sun! But then I have school right afterward, so I'm so tired."

## Dance, Dance, Dance!

When their weeks and months of practice give way to "dancing out," typically from May through September, morris teams are a study in almost perpetual, inexhaustible motion. But if you want to see where they're going in the ancient tradition, keep your eyes on the young ones.

"They like dancing. They really like dancing," says Rogers, speaking mostly of the teen And Sometimes Y group, to which many of the Johnny Jump Ups graduate. "I think they like participating on a team that's not competitive. There's not the intensity there would be on a sports team, but a lot of them take it very seriously and work really hard at it."

The enthusiasm of dancers on the other kids' teams is also noticeable.

"When we're on tour, it's all, 'Can I be in this dance?' If there are ten kids and we need six, I have to pick, but everyone wants to dance. I can think kids are sort of lukewarm at practice, but when it came to dancing out, they really wanted to dance."

Even when the adult dancers are hanging out after their May Day festivals—heading down to the Harp pub after Cushman or to Lady Killigrew after Montague, "the parents drink, but the kids aren't done with dancing yet . . . The adults are singing, but the kids want to dance, dance, dance!"

When she began teaching morris dancing to kids, Rogers was concerned about behavioral issues. "They want to dance. There are no issues at all," she says. Unlike adult members who sometimes have to be reminded during practice sessions to stop talking and pay attention, the Jump Ups "are interested in everything about it," including the tradition. "They're very enthusiastic."

While adult morris teams like Juggler Meadow and Wake Robin have their Harvest Ale around the region on Columbus Day weekend and the Marlboro Ale in southern Vermont on Memorial Day weekend, the Jump Ups head to Boston's Ginger Ale in Boston, as well as keeping their leaps and dances fresh at fairs around the region as schedules allow.

The last time Rogers went to the Marlboro Morris Ale five years ago, she noticed a new reality had begun visiting an old tradition. "It used to be all us, us, us," says the fifty-five-year-old Morris enthusiast. "Now there's a real representation of kids under twenty-one at the ale, singing the songs, leaping in the air. We're being eclipsed. It's what should be happening. It's really being passed on. And it's changing. They have their own identity. It's a living tradition."

**Nina Keller drives a Montague Farm commune tractor with, from left behind her, Richard Finestone, Tony Matthews, and John James**

# From News to New Age on Montague Farm

## May 1, 2009

*Although it drew much less national attention than the far larger Renaissance Community, earlier called Brotherhood of the Spirit, that attracted hundreds of young people to the area in the late 1960s and early 1970s, the Montague Farm commune intrigued me because of its political origins and ramifications nationally as well as the ways it dovetailed and interacted with the region's own sensibilities. It's one of the cultural touchstones I believe make this larger community what it is today.*

———

"Well, I think we ought to move the news service to a farm, somewhere in the hills, Canada perhaps—a place where people can begin to think clearly, a place to get all those city poisons out of their systems."

—Marshall Bloom, July 1968
co-founder, Liberation News Service

102

One evening 40 years ago, New York's Fillmore East rock venue filled for a preview showing of the Beatles' movie *Yellow Submarine* to benefit Liberation News Service. Meanwhile, 180 miles and light years away in Franklin County, movie audiences watched *The Thomas Crown Affair* and *Tammy and the Bachelor*.

What the New York crowd didn't realize was that the *Yellow Submarine* benefit was a pretext: the radical news service's founders were planning to use the money raised to move their operation—lock, stock, and printing presses—to a sixty-acre farm they'd secretly bought a four-hour drive away in Montague, Massachusetts.

That August 11, 1968 "heist"—the contents of LNS offices had already been loaded into a rental truck—was the birth of the Montague Farm about ten miles north of Amherst. The commune off North Leverett Road would soon became a pivotal outpost in that sixties generational push to get "back to the land" and became a pioneer in organic agriculture. It also ushered in the grass-roots anti-nuclear movement in the 1970s, in response to Northeast Utilities' plan to build twin reactors on the nearby Montague Plains.

The *Greenfield Recorder* had been running front-page stories about the Vietnam War and Richard Nixon's August 8 naming of Spiro Agnew as his vice-presidential running mate at the San Diego Republican Convention. But that August 13, readers also read about the battle that ensued in Montague when the LNS's New York contingent realized their presses and goods had been taken along with eleven thousand dollars in cash.

The explosion of headlines that followed in what had been quiet Franklin County reflected tensions that had been building during the increasingly radical 1960s.

Marshall Bloom, former editor of *The Amherst Student* newspaper at Amherst College, and Ray Mungo, editor of *Boston University News,* founded LNS in 1966 to report on the political battles at the time. Bloom was a veteran of the civil rights struggle in Selma, Alabama earlier in the decade. He'd helped lead a walkout of the 1966 commencement speech by Defense Secretary Robert McNamara at Amherst, then gotten thrown out of the London School of Economics and had his election to the American Student Press Association presidency rescinded after protesting the group's CIA funding. He'd enlisted Mungo's help setting up the press service to feed as many as four hundred alternative papers around the country.

"The service supplies New Left, hippie, and student papers with bits and pieces of news that may have been overlooked or misinterpreted' by daily newspapers and magazines," *Time* magazine reported in March 1968.

Over the next several months, as the nation recoiled from the assassinations of Martin Luther King and Bobby Kennedy and braced for confrontations at the Chicago Democratic convention in late August, LNS moved its headquarters from Washington, DC, to New York. Its own internal struggles reflected the fractious political climate of the times.

By August, Bloom, Mungo, and others who considered themselves the "virtuous caucus" were ready to leave behind those they considered the "vulgar Marxists" in New York who'd been rolling over them to make LNS a house organ for the more radical Students for a Democratic Society.

The somewhat woolier founders were ready to literally head to the hills for a quieter, more bucolic setting.

"The liberation we tried to force on the world became secondary to the liberation in our own lives," Mungo would write years later.

Mungo and a group of friends from Boston University, including that college newspaper's former poetry editor, Verandah Porche, had already made their move to a homestead they called Total Loss Farm, just over the Massachusetts line in Guilford, Vermont.

### Battle Lines

"Liberation News Rocked by Strife," reported the *New York Times* on August 15, 1968.

"An internal dispute at Liberation News Service, the left-wing news agency underground, and radical papers, broke into the open yesterday with charges of theft, embezzlement, and kidnapping."

Bloom and his friends were charged by LNS staff with taking "virtually everything we had, including a four-thousand-dollar offset press, typewriters, and files to the Montague farm Bloom had bought using five thousand dollars in embezzled LNS money," the *Times* reported.

Armed with baseball bats and with friends who were members of the Children of God rock band along with other toughs, the New

York contingent beat up Bloom, Mungo, and others in the Montague farmhouse through that Monday night just after the *Yellow Submarine* benefit. The night of post-heist battle, Mungo and Porche had driven down to Montague to welcome Bloom and the others to country living.

"There were suddenly five of us sitting on the bare floor surrounded by twice that number of armed Marxists," Mungo wrote in his 1970 book, *Famous Long Ago*.

"Meanwhile," he continued, "a thorough search-and-destroy mission was sweeping the house and barn. Somebody whom I did not recognize was dismantling the telephone. Chairs were overturned, furniture smashed, windows kicked in by zealous boots. Items and artifacts were scooped up. Three or four guys began to belt Bloom across the face, in the stomach, in the groin, while the rest of us watched from our little cell."

The confrontation continued on until morning, with Porche and a member of the rock band at one point singing "Amazing Grace." The whole night was laced with "a lot of theatrics," recalls Porche.

"One of the very important themes, in addition to ideological purity, was a kind of adventurism aimed at gaining credibility from Black people," says Porche, who still lives in Guilford. "A critique that Black leaders had, which was entirely correct, was that these white folks could get a haircut and make up with their parents and go home. So an important article of faith would be to commit violent acts to show that you couldn't go home, either. It was a very long night."

### Walking in Wonder

"I'd never been on a farm before," says founding member Harvey Wasserman, who had written for Liberation News Service from Chicago at the request of his boyhood friend Bloom. "We fell in love with the soil, with farming. It was a lot of work, but it was wonderful work. We were walking in wonder.

"For a lot of us who'd grown up in the cities and suburbs," he remembers, "we were completely blown away by how beautiful it was, continually, on a day-to-day basis. That was a big part of our later opposition to the proposed Montague Plains nuclear reactor, that that lump of pure ugliness was going to impose itself on this beautiful town was inconceivable."

"The phenomenon of this whole movement was the connection to nature," recalls Richard Wizansky, a founder of the Guilford commune and frequent visitor to Montague. "We all felt the gift of being here and the knowledge that here were a bunch of city folks living in nature. We could just look at the trees, and not have neighbors, and be in the healing bosom of the natural world. That was the lesson of the commune, I think: having to live by nature and living in nature."

The sense of wonder, though, gave way to the struggle that living in nature would mean for people who'd grown up in cities or suburbia.

Bloom and his friends had bought the Chestnut Hill farm while dedicated to continuing LNS. Then, reality set in: winter was coming, and they were hundreds of miles from the news sources that had been right out the door in New York and Washington. Their only easy contact to the outside world in Montague was the telephone, and they needed income to pay the bills while also getting wood ready for winter and figuring out how to farm.

"A lot of dawnings happened that winter," remembers Sam Lovejoy, an Amherst College friend of Bloom from outside Springfield who moved to the farm a year after the commune started up. "We got to figure out how to feed ourselves and support ourselves."

In *What the Trees Said,* his 1971 book about "life on a New Age farm," commune co-founder Steve Diamond wrote, "The main reason I wanted to stop printing Liberation News Service mailings was this: We simply didn't have anything more to say other than perhaps get some land, get your people together and see what happens.

"You see," Diamond continued, "one thing that we really hadn't considered when we planned to move to the country was the effect such a change would render unto our heads. We'd assumed it would be merely a geographic change. Who could have foreseen that our minds would be blown in the process?"

After several more months, the Montague-based news service ended that November when the ink in the press froze in the unheated barn. LNS continued in New York into the next year.

Help came from Lovejoy. He showed the others how to get farm equipment and get it to run. And inspiration came from women commune members who gravitated toward organic agriculture.

Montague Farm began growing cucumbers on a ten-acre patch of south-facing hillside that provided ideal conditions for organic practices. It was even visited by Robert Rodale Jr., who wrote in *Organic Gardening* about "America's new peasantry" in Montague. Bloom would drive a burlap bag of cucumbers to Oxford Pickle Company's Deerfield plant in his two-seat Triumph sedan to sell for twenty-five dollars a ton, remembers one former member.

At first, people came from around Franklin County to gawk at the long-haired strangers who looked just like the hippies TV and the national media had been depicting as consumed by "drugs, sex, and rock 'n' roll." Locals drove by the farm to gawk at the hippies and leer at the braless women, recalls Dan Keller. Yankee tolerance provided a laconic welcome for the new generation of workers.

"We were like a foreign body plunked down there," recalls Tom Fels, who moved to Montague in his last year at Amherst College and helps maintain a 1960s-era archive housed at the University of Massachusetts library. "We might have been a tribe of Africans or Eskimos—something that was totally different. We were bringing this urban countercultural energy to a place that hadn't seen it."

While there were plenty of young people experimenting with drugs and the sexual freedom of the times, they were also trying to connect with the environment and push for political change.

"We were very much experimenting with everything social, with everything political, with everything personal," says Susan Mareneck, a Smith College graduate who moved to the farm with her Amherst alumnus husband later in 1968. "We were inventing these lives not like our parents had led or led us to believe our lives should be."

Mareneck, who'd grown up in suburban Chicago, remembers, "Trying to figure out how to live in rural New England was such an education. Until I came to western New England, I never knew there was a white culture in America. In suburbia, I didn't have any connection to people's ethnicity, traditions, or ways of living."

She and other commune members tapped into the rhythm of the deeper community, connecting with old timers like Jacob Perkins, who made butter and lived in a house that "smelled like cream and milk." Other neighbors like Woody Brown, Stanley Podlenski, and Charlie Hepburn befriended the new arrivals despite frequent run-ins from town officials and spying missions by FBI agents, who'd been doing surveillance on LNS ever since its Washington days.

"We were rebelling against the status quo, going back to the land and publishing alternative newspapers, but in our hearts, I think we were trying to be good citizens," Mareneck says.

Toward that end, Lovejoy, Mareneck, and other members encouraged their friends to reach out to townsfolk more, even setting up a food concession at the Montague Inn for a while.

Fortunately, the arrival of those new-age farmers eager to work the land coincided perfectly with the increasing numbers of aging locals who had been lamenting their own offspring leaving their family farms.

Diamond, who died in 2006, wrote, "Almost all of Chestnut Hill was settled by the Ripley family, who built a great house and several others around here. But the children and their children moved away, and the farm, the house, and the sixty-acre piece of land were sold after Lucian Ripley, who lived here all alone, died of a stroke.

"The children went to the cities in search of homes heated at the flick of a switch," Diamond continued, "looking for a middle-class security that their farmer parents were never quite able to guarantee. And we, who are the children of the secure, find ourselves reclaiming that land, desirous of the poverty that keeps us free."

Lucian Ripley's brother Rob, who had sold off to the commune the Montague farm he'd been raised on, continued to live on his own place next door.

"He saw we were renovating it and were interested in his strawberry patch and his rhubarb," recalls Nina Keller, who moved to the Montague commune from one nearby in southern Vermont and eventually went on to a spin-off commune in Wendell, where she lives. "We were his sugaring crew. We were champing at the bit to be with him and soak up his Yankee knowledge and his experience."

Rob Ripley, who had sugared with horses until five years before Bloom and company arrived, told the *Recorder* in a 1991 interview, "I got along with them fine. They used to help me with sugaring for ten or fifteen years. It was the only help I had."

### Energized and Focused

Bloom struggled with manic depression as well as the stresses of being a closeted homosexual at a sexually liberating time when gay culture was just beginning to surface. He committed suicide in the fall of 1969 a few months after their Montague arrival. The suicide dealt a traumatic blow to friends of the twenty-five-year-old inspirational community co-founder.

Members arrived and left, in some cases abandoning their focus on farming and making a simple living in their rural outpost. Some, like Lovejoy, painted houses or worked at jobs at area daycare centers or sold vegetables.

Then, in 1973, Northeast Utilities announced plans to build twin nuclear reactors on the nearby Montague Plains, where the town had recently pushed back an effort by the Boston & Maine Railroad to build a dump for garbage from eastern Massachusetts. "Don't Upset Montague's Plains," read the bumper stickers, which newly arriving commune members mistook to reflect an environmental movement rather than native community pride, recalls Lovejoy.

Lovejoy, who was twenty-seven at the time, first saw the five-hundred-foot-tall weather-data tower he would later topple while being driven up Route 47 from Sunderland after a visit to the West Coast in early 1964.

"I remember my first words were, 'Somebody's going to knock that down.'"

Lovejoy had been a physics and math major at Amherst College before switching his studies to political science.

"That was half the reason the nuke didn't bother me," he says looking back on his pre-Montague days. "I had just never looked at the negatives."

From the moment that commune members heard about plans for the reactors, they were incensed—as though the political foes from their urban LNS days had followed them to their rural doorstep.

"It immediately energized and focused us," remembers Wasserman. "There never was a doubt. From the instant I saw the photograph (a rendering of the plant) in the *Recorder*, I knew we were going to fight it and win."

Earlier, Wasserman remembers being a supporter of nuclear power as a "technical fix" to the nation's energy crisis that had reared its head in 1973.

Anna Gyorgy, who'd moved to Montague from New York in 1971 for a decade, remembers reading about the planned reactor the same week she discovered John Goffman's *Poison Power*. She brought the book home so she could read up on a subject she knew nothing about and discuss it with others around the dinner table.

"It was a new family project," says Gyorgy, who went on to write her own 1979 book, *No Nukes: Everyone's Guide to Nuclear Power* and then head Ralph Nader's Critical Mass Energy Project. "Our focus had been to stay alive and keep this communal thing going. I'd been there three years. We were quite rooted there and felt really secure in our work and the need to protect our community from that threat."

Lovejoy walked onto the Montague Plains early on the morning on February 22, 1974 and, using a few simple tools, loosened several turnbuckles to remove the tower's guy wires and topple it. Then, he turned himself in to police.

"I thought people would say, 'Wow, he turned himself in.' So many people got hung up on the fact I'd destroyed property, I thought my police statement had sort of cured that problem. People were hung up on property. We were willing to share our property, so we didn't look on it as anything."

Lovejoy, charged with malicious destruction of personal property, defended himself in Franklin County Superior Court, winning on a technicality.

His Washington's Birthday act of civil disobedience—documented in *Lovejoy's Nuclear War*, a Green Mountain Post film made by Light and Dan Keller—was the chop heard round the world. It led to a chilling of relations between commune members and townspeople but also to a campaign to educate people in the area about the dangers of nuclear power.

The twin-reactor Montague nuclear project was canceled by Northeast Utilities in 1980.

The opposition spearheaded by the Montague Farm became a rallying point that helped give birth to a national antinuclear movement. A highlight was a September 1979 No Nukes benefit concert that included Jackson Browne, Graham Nash, James Taylor, and Bonnie Raitt in Madison Square Garden—a harkening back to Liberation News Service's New York connection.

Locally, the farm-spawned No Nukes movement included political mobilization with Gyorgy running for selectboard and Keller and

Lovejoy running for town meeting member seats on the NO—Nuclear Opposition—Party ticket.

Farm members also set up the Alternative Energy Coalition, with offices in Turners Falls and then Greenfield, inspiring the Clamshell Alliance to fight the planned reactor in Seabrook, New Hampshire.

Many of those Seabrook activists came from or wound up in the area around Montague.

### A Very Real Family

Four decades after its founding, the effects of the Montague Farm are still felt by those who lived there as well as in the community. In 2005, it was sold to become a spiritual center run by the nonprofit Zen Peacemakers Community to carry on many of the commune's original values. The handwritten sign, "Better active today than radioactive tomorrow" is still there on the once-weathered barn, which has been spruced up beyond any commune member's wildest sixties hallucination.

Some farm members have died. Others have moved elsewhere. Still others, like Lovejoy, the Kellers, and Tony Matthews in Gill, have become active in municipal affairs.

Less than a mile away from the farm, where North Leverett has also become home to two Buddhist temples, Mareneck lives in the home that once served as the commune's overflow annex.

Commune members didn't just learn from blacksmith Joe Eberlein, who worked down the road, or from neighbors like Verne and Katy Aiken, she recalls. "We also learned from our time together. Those people are still my family in the world, a very real family. That experience really altered our lives for many of us. Many of our lives have been devoted to bringing a different consciousness about living to whatever it is we did. I think we're applying to the world some of the lessons we all learned there."

Those lessons were about the importance of interdependent community relationships.

"That's especially important as we're jettisoned into this age, as I've found working with my church and nonprofits in New York," says Mareneck, who volunteers to work on prison reform there. "Can we really do it if not all together? If we do it without being together, what will we have accomplished? We can't be okay if everybody isn't okay."

If Bloom and his Liberation New Service friends were able to feel at home here because of a tradition of tolerance and a streak of Daniel Shays independence, "it's a mutually reinforcing situation," says Nina Keller, who remains at sixty-two an active organic gardener at the Wendell communal farm. She's also a vocal opponent of the Vermont Yankee nuclear plant. "There's been great political continuity, and it's still moving on."

Her sixty-year-old husband, Dan, believes the Montague Farm "brought a level of awareness of nuclear power that changed the town forever. LNS opened the community up to a lot of different waves of thought that weren't topics for discussion. Having the radical perspective that was being promulgated on Chestnut Hill opened the eyes of people in Franklin County to the problems of the war and the nuclear thing and to organic gardening."

Lovejoy, who at sixty-two lives on Main Street in Montague Center and has served as a selectboard member and even as a regional planning board chairman, believes Montague Farm provided a "lightning bolt of idealism" for the town.

"And there's nothing better than to have a little idealism show up. A lot of issues that we believed in and people thought might be slightly crazy, or at least slightly impractical, came to be. They're now mainstream. America has changed. This community has changed. In many ways, they've caught up with us. But in many ways, we had a lot to learn from them, so we had to catch up to the community."

Gyorgy, now sixty-one, who came to Montague from a master's program at Barnard College that "had no relationship to ecology," says, "What appealed to me was living your values without having money as the main concern."

Returning to live on the Wendell farm after years of organizing in Germany around issues of women and ecology, she adds, "Here we were really wanting to put our principles into practice. In terms of a new-age family, I think we did it."

Wasserman, the sixty-two-year-old boyhood friend of commune co-founder Bloom, has written five books on politics and lives in Columbus, Ohio. "Throughout every minute of the fourteen years I was at Montague, I was aware it was an incredibly special experience, both personally and historically—that it was a shining moment for all of us that would have a lasting impact on the world," he says.

"And it did, because it continues. Because it shows what's possible."

the fourteenth Dalai Lama, left, and Paul "Tiny" Stacy

# A Big Man, A Bigger Heart

## December 5, 2007

*For anyone who sees the Tibetan stone structure along Routes 5 and 10 in Deerfield, Massachusetts, its hidden story may come as a surprise, as the announcement of its dedication certainly did to me. Even more surprising is to learn about someone as colorful as Tiny Stacy, who had an open heart and a spirit so playful that he wrestled and laughed with the Dalai Lama, thus discovering a bit of himself in the process.*

Paul Stacy was as large as life. The six-foot, four-inch mountain of a man, it seemed, was the perfect bodyguard and driver for the fourteenth Dalai Lama, whose visit to the Pioneer Valley the past week marked in some ways an important milestone for the region's Tibetan community.

Yet Tiny—as the three-hundred-pound giant was affectionately known to an astonishing array of people—also lived life to the fullest right up to his death in 1994 after years of drug and alcohol abuse, as well as battling diabetes and its complications.

As a grand part of the fullness of his life, he immersed himself in Buddhist meditation with the Dalai Lama and other teachers in his later years.

Tiny was grand, as well, in the way he embraced the world just as he physically hugged those around him—including the Dalai Lama and the people he came to know through his family's Blue Plate Lounge in Holden, Massachusetts: singer Arlo Guthrie, author Ram Dass, poet Lawrence Ferlinghetti, Grateful Dead members Mickey Hart and Bob Weir, and Woodstock's Wavy Gravy.

That embrace meant donations to survival centers, benefit concerts for the homeless, work to help Tibetan refugees, and meditation sessions for recovering alcoholics and substance abusers. It's because of those works that Tibetan stonemason Sonam Lama began work one recent morning on a Buddhist shrine, or stupa, for Tiny in Deerfield. At his side was a friend of Tiny's, Steven Rodman of Greenfield, who is helping with the project and having it documented by filmmaker Carlyn Saltman of Turners Falls.

Shortly after 8 AM, in light rain, the Deerfield stonemason broke ground in front of Sonam Lama's recently opened shopping plaza off Routes 5 and 10. Exactly between flagpoles where the American banner and a Tibetan prayer flag fly, Sonam is building the stone memorial, which he estimates will be ten feet in diameter and maybe twelve feet high.

In front of his eclectic plaza, which incorporates Tibetan prayer wheels and traditional painting in its architecture, the 1989 refugee intentionally waited until after the Dalai Lama's departure from the area Thursday to begin working on the stupa to avoid any confusion that his purpose is to show appreciation for Tiny.

"Not only Tiny but many Americans helped Tibetans and (would) help anybody who needs help," says Sonam, who met Stacy in Amherst soon after arriving in the area in 1986. "He was one really neat guy. He was so compassionate," Sonam says of the self-described ski bum turned spiritual seeker.

Tiny would give him loads and loads of old clothes he'd collected to take to the Amherst Survival Center, and helped him find masonry customers, including Peter, Paul, and Mary member Mary Travers at her Connecticut home.

"Before he died, I saw him in Middlebury, Vermont, on crutches, guarding the Dalai Lama. He was a very caring person. I wished I could do something for him, because he was so nice for so many people."

## Like a Rivulet

Tiny Stacy, born on Groundhog Day, 1944, was "always the center of gravity," says Rodman, who met him in 1971 soon after arriving in Worcester from San Francisco. "Everybody was a friend of Tiny's. He made you feel, no matter who you were, you were his closest friend."

Stacy worked as a bartender at the Blue Plate on Route 122A, which he turned into a haven for lovers of music and poetry on a scale as huge as Tiny himself. Country Joe McDonald, the New Riders of the Purple Sage, and Arlo Guthrie all flocked there. Poet Allen Ginsberg wrote to Tiny about doing a reading there but never made it.

In the spirit of the time, Rodman remembers, he listened with Stacy to tapes of Tibetan chanting—something that had sent Tiny into checking out all he could about altered states of consciousness other than the drugs and alcohol he'd been abusing, by connecting with Carlos Castaneda, Buddhism, martial arts, and eventually the His Holiness himself.

When the supreme Tibetan spiritual leader spoke at Amherst College in 1979, college dropout Stacy was there and became so enthralled that he turned out the following night to hear him at Harvard University. And even though he was still "in the grip of the grape," the gentle big man decided when he heard about the Dalai Lama's return a couple of years later that he'd offer to work as his bodyguard.

That meant drying out at a New Hampshire retreat, where he meditated, recalls Rodman.

Stacy continued bringing food to the elderly and organizing benefits to help Vietnam vets.

"He'd move wherever he could help the most," Rodman remembers. "He was like water, like a rivulet."

Six weeks after getting out of the hospital in New Hampshire, Stacy's bushy, grey-bearded friend recalls, Tiny was driving the Dalai Lama in his Tiny-sized car and serving as official chauffeur. Both men, strikingly similar as humble, compassionate, and light-hearted human beings, hit it off "like brothers separated at birth."

It sounds hard to believe, but en route from the Adirondacks to Boston on their first detail together, the two stopped off at a Howard Johnson's on the Mass Pike to split a frankfurter because the Tibetan leader says he wondered what Americans really eat.

Even more incredibly, Rodman says the Dalai Lama and Tiny wrestled in a playful way that suggested that the statesman in exile, hailed at age two as Tenzin Gyatso, the fourteenth leader of Tibet, was happy to simply find a kindred soul with whom he could play despite their vastly different corporeal manifestations.

At the same time, Rodman says of Stacy, "His love and respect for the Dalai Lama was as big as Tiny was," and meeting the spiritual leader helped him find what he had been searching for in life.

"Buddhism certainly helped him more with depression than drugs ever did. He was like a thirsty man who was searching. He finally found the real deal."

Tiny, shown with the Dalai Lama in the documentary *Heart of Tibet* and included in Ram Dass's book, *How Can I Help? Stories and Reflections on Service,* deepened his own spiritual practice. It helped him as he helped substance abusers and took a job as a substance-abuse counselor at Massachusetts Correctional Institution, Shirley.

"Tiny took care of everybody in the world but himself," observes Rodman. "His path of compassion allowed him to let go of his own personal stuff."

## A Peaceful, Loving Soul

Sonam Lama called on fourteen Tibetan monks to dedicate the site of Tiny's stupa in February, asking permission of the spirits believed to live at the site to erect a shrine there that will be filled with thousands of written mantras, wrapped in white cloth, as well as holy soil, rocks, tools, and other ritual objects.

Sonam has been planning the stupa for nearly ten years, first near his home when he lived in Greenfield. When he bought the former Deerfield motel property, he decided that would be a more visible site.

The forty-six-year-old stonemason has built stupas in New York, Vermont, and Chicago—including one for actor Richard Gere who, like seemingly everyone, knew Tiny.

When he returned from a visit to Nepal last month, Sonam had a Tibetan-made brass sun and moon—traditional symbols to cap a stupa—sent back. The sun, cradled in the moon, will become part of the final work along with an umbrella symbol created by Ashfield blacksmith Steve Smithers.

Sonam figures it will take a couple of weeks to finish building the stupa and that he will ask a high monk to consecrate it by the end of summer. Along the way, videographer Saltman will document the process and interview some of the many friends of Tiny.

Like all stupas, Sonam says, this will be a place for healing and prayer, a peaceful place. Tiny, whom it's meant to honor, would have liked such a place, and there will be a marker telling people about him. In another way, though, the stupa may represent that the Pioneer Valley's Tibetan community has come into its own in the past decade and a half, says Rodman. In showing appreciation for Tiny, he says, the monument will also be an expression of gratitude toward others who helped the community get established.

The stone stupa will be a permanent marker of respect, much like the white cloth kata, or scarf, wrapped around Tiny's neck after his death. It had been placed there a few months earlier by the Dalai Lama himself with a long, emotional embrace and the words, "This knot unites you and I together forever."

*photo by Chuck Blake*

**Gerry Allen with his dairy cows**

# Not a Discouraging Word Is Herd

### August 21, 1980

*"Dairy farming is so satisfying," Conway farmer John Wholey told me in 2009. "Life is beating the hell out of us, but we've seen all the good stuff, like if you deliver a calf or you look back down the length of the barn and all the cows are standing there feeding, and it's just a nice thing."*

*One of my greatest joys as a reporter was discovering the complex wonders of dairy farming, sometimes through extended visits with people for whom I had the greatest respect and admiration, dairy farmers like Gary Allen, Wholey, and others who labored so hard for so little money doing work they loved. They inspired me with their patience and determination.*

———

Young Wayne Allen steps onto a mud-stained footstool and reaches up to plug the long, black, plastic hose into the pipe that runs along the white wooden ceiling.

118

It's 5:45 AM. Forty-five minutes after waking, while most other twelve-year-olds sleep, the pint-sized dairyman helps milk the family Holsteins at Gully Glen Dairy Farm.

The pump on the pipeline, helping draw milk from the udders of the cows just in from pasture, ticks like a loud clock.

The forty-four black-and-white cows, oblivious to the flurry of human activity around them, munch casually on hard, green, dehydrated alfalfa cubes, their tails occasionally swinging in time with the pulsating pump.

Tick. Tock. Tick. Tock. Swish, swish.

"This is when I like to do all my thinking," says Wayne's father, Gerry Allen, who has just placed the pipes of the milking machine on the udder of a cow. "This is where I dream up all my plans for expansion. They don't always go over too good when I bring them up for discussion at the supper table," he laughs.

The voice of the thirty-six-year-old farmer barely carries over the roar of four fans, which blow all day to keep the milking herd cool and production up.

Across the thirty-six-stall barn from his son, Allen sits on a seat attached to his waist and resting on a spring-tipped pedestal.

The farmer wears Western-style boots, jeans, a sleeveless print shirt, a religious medal across his chest, a red cap over his black hair, and a green belt attached to the seat that accompanies him from cow to cow.

"I have two goals," he says. "The first is to have the top herd in Franklin County. The second is to have the top herd in Massachusetts."

Three of the bare incandescent bulbs overhead light the milking process.

Allen pulls a paper towel from the wall, dips it in a bucket of rinse, and wipes the udder. He attaches the machine, then waits as it pumps warm milk into the tank in the adjoining milkhouse. After maybe seven minutes, he removes the siphons and attaches them to the next cow, which he's just prepared. He takes a plastic bottle of purple lanolin rinse and dips the nipples of the animal that has just been milked.

The cow is oblivious.

The process repeats itself over and over, father and son working down the two lines of cattle accompanied by the steady tick-tock pulse of the milking machine.

"The time spent with the cows is time well-spent," says Allen. "That's where you make your living. You can buy feed a hell of a lot cheaper than you can buy equipment and rent land."

That's why the farm switched this year to green alfalfa cubes from northern Vermont.

Allen figured he can buy the cubes much cheaper than he could grow his own hay and, thus, put his own time to better use around the barn.

"Running around trying to make hay is like throwing money in the brook," he says, plugging the hose in further down the line of cattle.

He has already sold much of his haymaking equipment and reduced the land he rents from his neighbor by twenty acres.

Gully Glen consists of approximately 140 acres, 60 of which are rented. There are 73 acres of feed corn and hay acreage as well.

"I don't think I know as much as these farmers who've been farming for twenty years. But I'm better off staying home tending the cows instead of running all that equipment."

It is eight o'clock. Gerry Allen and two of his sons have come into the farmhouse, leaving their boots behind in the mudroom and tossing their caps on an old, disconnected wood stove.

Joined by a third son, they sit together around the rectangular breakfast table at one end of the large kitchen. In the middle of the room is an enormous wood stove which in winter heats the entire farmhouse. In their spare time, Allen and his three boys are rebuilding the foundation of the house.

"It's 125 years old . . . but we'll get it fixed someday," he says.

Rather than sit down, Ann Marie Allen waits on the rest of the family. She has made two and a half dozen muffins, using the last of the blueberries she froze a year ago. There are eggs, too, and bacon, milk, juice, and coffee.

With the boys home for the summer and Wayne helping with the milking, it's the first time in their eight years on the farm that the thirty-eight-year-old woman has been able to devote time to running the house. "Every year the boys get older, the easier it gets," says their father. "As they get older, it evens out the responsibility all the way around.

Scott, 16; David, 15, and Wayne admit their father works them hard. But they don't mind, they say.

"It's the best way to bring up three boys," Allen says. "I won't say they all want to be working on a dairy farm when they get older. But I hope they do."

Scott and Wayne are up every morning at five, milking the cows and sweeping the barn. David doesn't wake up until eight, but there are already plans to have him do the 1 AM milking when the family changes its schedule in September.

"We'll be able to get five or six hours' sleep that won't be broken up, Allen predicts.

They plan to go to three milkings a day, a change they hope will boost production—2,500 pounds—roughly 315 gallons, a day—by 15 percent and help pay for the new sixty-foot-high silo that's due to be delivered the following day.

"We try to keep expenses down," Allen explains. "You can control expenses if you sit down and figure long enough. We usually hash things over. We try to include the boys. I guess the best piece of equipment we own is a nineteen-dollar calculator."

Wayne, who has been doing chores since he was seven, is serious and silent until asked a question.

photo by Chuck Blake

**breakfast at the Allen table**

121

"When I first came, I didn't like the cows," he says quietly. "I didn't want to get near them because they were bigger than me."

Now, says Wayne, who plans to become a veterinarian eventually, "I like just being with the animals. Most kids just walk the street. I have something to do right here."

Of his school classmates, the seventh grader says, "When I want to talk about farming, they're not interested. They're more interested in sports."

Wayne is the animal lover. His brothers are machinery-minded.

For their hard work feeding the cattle and running heavy machinery, Scott and David each earn forty dollars a week, and Wayne gets twenty-five dollars of every milk check.

Their father, sitting at the table in his stocking feet, has never considered how the farm would operate without the three young hands.

"It was always based on the idea the boys were going to help."

Until eight years ago, when he bought the eighty-acre farm between Leyden Road and the Green River a half-mile south of the Leyden line, Allen was a tractor-trailer driver in his native Bernardston.

He had a few cows and a few pigs but was working for someone else, and that hurt. "We were spinning our wheels and getting nowhere," he recalls.

"I grew up around farming," says Allen, mulling over his youth when he helped a neighboring farmer.

"I thought it was a good way of life," he says. "My impression of farming was a lot different than when I bought this farm. The dairy industry was in a slump when I bought this place. It was nothing but an uphill battle."

The farm—without cows and equipment—cost sixty-five thousand dollars, and another thirty-five thousand dollars, Allen figures, was needed to start up.

"You can't buy a good farm today for less than $165,000. I dare say that doesn't include cattle and everything."

But he adds, "If you want to go after it and want it bad enough, you can't let those figures scare you. No one was encouraging me. What helped me more than anything was when people said I couldn't do it. I've made the investment. I guess I'm going to stay here."

When he started out with twenty-five head—there are nearly seventy today—Allen was recovering from an accident in which a hay baler had almost torn off his arm. Wayne was only five, and Ann was doing much of the milking. The inside of the barn had to be rebuilt, the tank had to be replaced, the gutter cleaner and pipeline had to be overhauled.

But he says, "You can't be afraid to borrow. If I waited to put enough money away to buy that silo, I'd be in the old age home." He smiles broadly and shrugs his shoulders.

The Allens also plan to put up a new barn and buy a bigger milk tank this fall, so they can begin milking fifty cows in October.

In his 13-hour-day, 365-day-a-year job, Allen earns between $7,500 and $8,500 a year. That's what's left from a gross income of more than $100,000.

"It's not like a five-day-a-week job, and we don't have as much money in our pockets," says the farmer. "But we're still better off 'cause we're building equity. We don't have much left over at the end of the year. But we're worth more each year on paper. I still owe bills, I still owe money. We're getting organized."

Farming is a day in, day out struggle, says the former truck driver—a new challenge each day.

"I don't feel like we're in a rut at all. I feel like we're moving up," he says, wiping his brow with a red handkerchief.

"I wouldn't give it up for anything. There's a lot of discouraging days. But we manage to overcome them."

It is 10:15 in the morning when Larry Newton arrives. He is wearing galoshes and green work clothes bearing the same Eastern logo that is on Gerry Allen's cap. Newton, in fact, is wearing an identical cap and brings with him a third cap——a new one, for which he will charge Allen $2.80.

Already today, Allen has overseen the unloading of twenty-four tons of lime.

And in what will be the most revolting chore of the day, Allen has removed the afterbirth from the uterus of Eve, who gave birth to a calf a week and a half ago.

Newton's visit promises future calves, however, and the Eastern logo, which incorporates the likeness of a calf, represents the Eastern Artificial Insemination Cooperative.

In the rear of his grey Toyota is the reproductive equivalent of twenty bulls. The Allens, after reviewing the descriptions of forty sires in an Eastern booklet, have settled on Wimson Executive, a twenty-four-hundred-pound stud from Williamson, New York.

Allen and his son Wayne go through the illustrated sire book often to choose which sire's traits would best match those of a particular cow.

In the milkhouse, the technician writes out a receipt for fourteen dollars——eight dollars for the semen and six dollars for the service call—and attaches a seven-inch plastic straw to what appears to be a two-foot-long rod. Newton proceeds to the barn, where he inserts the rod into one of the cows, Oleo. She has never been bred before. In less than sixty seconds, the rod is removed and Newton is ready to repeat the process for Joan.

Neither cow gives the slightest indication that anything out-of-the-ordinary is taking place.

Newton is not out of the yard five minutes before a red truck enters. A sign on the truck reads C.P. ZIMMERMAN AND SONS, CATTLE DEALERS, LEYDEN.

It is 10:40. Driver Billy Zimmerman jumps down. With Gerry and Scott Allen, he walks around to a small deteriorating shed beside the barn to fetch Jill.

The cow aborted a calf a few months ago and is going dry. She is to be sold, so Zimmerman attaches a yellow tag to her right ear—an abrupt action that causes her to jerk slightly.

Zimmerman ties a rope around her head and neck. He and Scott pull the cow onto the truck as Allen and Wayne heave mightily from behind.

The cow is aboard. Zimmerman and Allen shut the back door. The red truck whisks out of the yard five minutes after it entered.

At eleven o'clock, Scott drags a hose from outside the milkhouse to a barn stall where Rachel has been brought in.

It's a case of foot rot, and the Allens, being their own veterinarians, have improvised their own experimental treatment.

Allen lifts Rachel's left rear leg, ties a rope to it, then attaches a pulley to a hook inserted into the roof over the kicking bovine. The pulley is attached to the rope, and Gerry hoists Rachel's leg.

"It's just like athlete's foot," he says, spraying the cleave of the hoof with water as Wayne holds onto the rope. "We've had a lot of trouble with this because the ground's so dry. This is a little crude, but it works," Allen laughs. "We usually stick the foot in a pail of water and the pail gets knocked over a couple of times."

The farmer opens a container of a sloppy green gel, and with his finger applies the medication to the animal's hoof.

Then he wraps the hoof in a plastic bag marked "six deli bagels" and ties it with twine. A plastic bread bag is then wrapped around and tied with twine.

"There you go, toots," says the farmer, letting her foot down easily.

Rain clouds have blanketed the sky over the farm and beyond the Green River over the nearby hills of Colrain and Shelburne.

"I hope it rains," Gerry Allen says, shaking his head. "That corn really needs rain."

Looking out over the farm, he sees the cows out in the field in bovine relaxation.

"Hey, Scott," he calls out suddenly, "give those cows something to eat. I can't stand to see those cows not eating. If they haven't got something right in front of them, I'm not happy."

It's 11:55, and Allen is ripe for another project: pulling the handmade wagon the family made last summer off its running gear so the bottom can be used for a new feed wagon.

Scott Allen mans the bucket loader, which carries a few cement blocks, some wooden planks, and a long piece of chain to be used in the chore.

The sky is charcoal grey. It begins to rain gently. The only sounds are in the distance: the pattering of raindrops, the chirping of birds, whirring of barn fans.

After several attempts to hoist the wagon with the bucket loader and insert the blocks as supports, David Allen, driving the tractor, pulls the running gear out from under the wagon to separate the two parts.

"Let's get our stuff and get out of here," calls Allen to his boys, running toward the house in what's now a downpour. "It's dinner time, and I'm hungry."

The rain slows the day. Back in the farmhouse kitchen, lunch—consisting of spaghetti and meatballs—lasts from 12:30 until 2:30 PM, when the rain begins to taper off.

Wearing dry shirts, the three head back outside.

David Allen heads off in the tractor to chop hay for the cattle's evening meal.

Gerry, Scott, and Wayne Allen pile into the pickup truck to take a look at how their corn is doing.

The truck moves slowly down the rutted dirt path bordered on both sides by cornfields.

Past the road, which leads to Camp Kee-Wan-Nee and past the town farm, is a fifteen-acre patch of corn on one side, an eighteen-acre patch on the other.

"Holy Christ, how it's grown," exclaims Gerry Allen, surveying the damp acreage as rain continues to fall. He brings the vehicle to a halt and says to Wayne, "Go stand next to it and let's see how it's doing."

Gerry Allen climbs down, too, and stands next to his son, who is half as tall as the crop. With a measuring stick, he tries to reach the top to measure accurately.

The corn, some of its leaves withered from the recent dry spell, is nine feet tall and starting to "ear out."

In less than a month, it will be cutting time.

But now, as the truck pulls back into the yard, it's chore time, and the boys begin feeding the hungry cattle again.

It's still raining, so Gerry dons a black raincoat that's been hanging in the work shed.

At three, a man in his fifties in a copper-colored van pulls into the yard and steps down.

"How do you do, sir?" asks the man wearing a light blue shirt, white pants, and red cap topping short white hair. "Bernie McLaughlin, McLaughlin Equipment Company," he introduces himself. "You've got yourself a nice little farm here."

Before long, the two men retreat from the rain into the work shed, an unlit extension of the barn where the Allens keep the hundred little odds and ends to repair equipment. McLaughlin sells the same nuts and bolts, but that isn't why he's come all the way from Southwick.

The salesman has heard the Allens were looking at silos, but upon arriving this soggy afternoon, he learns the family has already ordered one.

He is disturbed, and it registers in his gravelly voice and on his face. What makes the matter more disturbing is that Allen has just bought the same silo McLaughlin is offering, a Madison Super Harvester, but from another dealer. Allen is already sold on a high-moisture feeding program, which will require a second, smaller silo eventually.

But whereas the salesman thinks Allen should begin using high-moisture corn and put up the second silo immediately, the dairyman wants to wait a few months.

"I've got two goals in mind," the farmer tells the salesman, "to have the best herd in Franklin County and to have the best herd in Massachusetts. I know what I want to do. I just don't want to do too much at one time."

"You can't do anything in life without some goals," the salesman adds, studying the concrete floor.

"We're trying to move up, but we're trying to do so economically so these boys will have something when they take over. If there's one thing I'm proud of, it's that we've done it on our own."

The men slowly walk outside into the yard in the shadow of the large barn door with an eagle depicted over it.

The rain has stopped. The salesman's copper van pulls out of the yard at 4:15, just in time for the Allens to begin milking.

### Pulsating and Relaxing

The day ends as it began.

Milking is the crucial ritual for a dairy farmer. It cannot be avoided.

The fans are still roaring. The pipeline is pulsating again. The cows haven't budged from their stalls. All the bare, incandescent bulbs are lit.

Gerry Allen straps his portable milking stool to his waist. The scene is a replay from eleven hours earlier. But now, the gutters are full of manure, its pungent odor much more intense.

Now, too, the entire family is involved.

Wayne Allen milks the same side of the barn he worked on earlier.

"When I get a little bigger and can reach the stall cocks (pipeline inserts), I can milk both sides," the boy says eagerly. "I won't be lugging the stool all around."

His father, too, is milking, mulling over the salesman's visit as he does. That is how he learns about different ways of operating, about new methods and new equipment.

Allen's wife, Ann, who milked two or three years back, when she also worked in a feed store, will begin milking again next month, when the planned expansion requires a third daily milking.

"It's relaxing," she says. "It lets you unwind."

David Allen and his mother rake the manure from the stalls into the gutter, sweep the bedding, and prepare to clean out the barn. Using the bucket loader, Scott Allen brings discarded feed to the herd outside.

By 6:20, the milking process—tick-tock, tick-tock; udder wash, milking machine, after rinse; tick-tock, tick-tock—is complete.

David is on the tractor, bringing green-chop hay out to the cattle in the yard. Older brother Scott helps unload it from the wagon.

"They love that stuff," says Gerry Allen, watching his boys from the barn.

Within a half hour, Scott and Wayne unlock the heads of the barns' grand dames, who have been locked in place for more than half a day. The liberated cows leave languidly.

Suddenly, as if the departure of the slow-moving cattle has cleared the barn of any lethargy, the remaining half hour's activity is like Hurricane Elsie.

The fans are shut off. Gerry flicks a switch that starts the conveyer belt cleaning the gutter. Scott and Ann sweep up some of the bedding in the stalls. They carry out half a dozen or so thirty-pound bags of alfalfa briquettes for the next morning.

David is outside to make sure the manure—emptied slowly by the gutter cleaner—falls properly into the wagon. In a few minutes, he will bring the load to the hayfield where it will be spread.

Scott spreads a can of barn-grit lime around the barn so the cows will not slip when they enter in the morning.

"Fog 'em time," Gerry calls out at 7:10. The barn is empty except for the sleeveless farmer.

The fogger hisses as he turns it on, filling air with a mist.

"This helps production," says Gerry Allen. "They don't swat flies all day long because there are no flies in here to swat."

Holding his breath as he leaves the barn, he disconnects the fogger. The Allens begin showering before a supper of hot dogs. David pulls into the yard with an empty manure cart.

Tomorrow will be eventful in its own way.

Whitney, the milk transporter, will be over in the morning to haul the milk—five thousand pounds of it. Agway will deliver the silo. And maybe some more of the house foundation can be done or the chain saw fixed.

Gerry Allen heads inside for dinner. He shrugs his shoulders, smiles and reflects, "You can do a lot worse things than farming."

## July 15, 1989

Other than the blue silo rising up sixty feet beyond the barn, there's one noticeable change at the farm nearly nine years later: a forty-two-foot-long semitrailer hooked up to a white cab with the passenger door marked GK ALLEN.

After arriving at the house from the northern fields on a red International Farmall tractor, Gerry Allen is checking phone messages. His three sons grown and working off the farm, his wife now working in a Turners Falls bank, Allen depends on an answering machine to collect instructions about whether he'll be driving a load of wood chips to a paper mill in Maine, New York, or New Hampshire.

"That's how I subsidize our income," says Allen, 45. "It's almost essential today that a guy has something. All I know how to do is raise cows and drive a truck."

Soon, as he hauls an orange cart of wood shavings from a pile to the thirty-six stalls in the barn, Allen confesses, "I'd like to think of this farm as a little better showplace than it is. I haven't reached all of my goals yet. The economics wouldn't let me. I've had to put some of my plans on hold."

In about four hours, he will be joined by Scott, 25, who works on the farm milking at 4:30 AM before going to his job as a mason's assistant and then again afterward, sometimes until 7 or 8. He also works all day Saturday.

"With Scott here, we're on our way back," he says confidently. "He's taken hold of the herd, does all the breeding herd check and culling heifers. At either one end of the day or the other, he milks, so that if I leave at ten or eleven at night and get back at eight he does the milking."

With milk prices sinking, the farm had to boost its herd from forty-four in 1980 up to seventy-two. It was Scott who helped the farm scale back its herd to roughly fifty cows a few years ago to become more efficient.

"It was getting too much," says his father. "It just about killed me. He started culling and got rid of a lot of heifers. We cut labor and feed costs while maintaining the same production."

129

Allen's clearly happy to have his son's help, particularly after a six-month spell when Scott moved away because of the pressures of working that closely and intensely with the family.

Gerry Allen has been hauling chips three times a week for Roberts Brothers Lumber and has put in his bid for two more mills. That required four additional trailers, so Allen took out a ten-thousand-dollar loan.

With all five trailer trucks now running, he expects to be driving truck nearly every night of the week.

"When that truck's running strong, it carries half the debt load of this farm. I call that good income."

If overnight hauling followed by a twelve-hour day of farming, sounds intense, it's a vast improvement over last fall when he was hauling potatoes from the New Brunswick border to places like Buffalo, New York or Scranton, Pennsylvania.

"I'd leave here at seven o'clock Sunday and be back Thursday," he recalls. "You take what you can get."

The trucking income definitely helps, he says.

"Some guys sell a little extra hay, they sell maple syrup, or they sell vegetables. Ten years ago, we got by milking cows."

Ann Marie Allen, his wife, has gone to work as a teller and trainer at Bank of America.

"When I'm not here, she's up with Scotty at 4 AM feeding the calves, helping clean the stables, whatever's got to be done. You'd still call it a family affair. All the guys I know have a wife who helps out."

Son Wayne, 21, works on construction, lives at home and often helps out weekends doing carpentry around the farm.

David, 24, lives in Millers Falls, married, with two children, and helps out three or four times a week, including Saturdays.

The plan is to have David, who drives a tank truck nights, help with an expanded family trucking business. In the fall, he helps chop corn.

"David would like to farm, says Gerry. "But we can't quite generate enough income to support a farm of this size. Farms can't pay the wages that everybody else can."

The pay Scott gets is about minimum wage, but it means that his father doesn't have to hire someone to do the work.

In 1980, the Allen farm was one of about 125 dairy farms in the county. Now, it's one of only four in Greenfield, and about 40 have dropped out around the county.

"It's turned into more a way of life than a way of living," he explains. "It's kind of pathetic. Everything's gone up except the price of milk. We've hit rock bottom with the milk market."

And then he adds, ever hopeful, "It should turn around in the next month."

Less than half a mile from the old Greenfield Poor Farm, which a farmer named Justin Root gave the town in 1849 and became in 2011 Just Roots / Greenfield Community Farm through the vision of a new crop of young farmers, Gerry Allen imagines a sense of renewal:

"You'd be surprised at the young folks who left the farm and are coming back," he says, rarely stopping work for a minute as he talks. "It's in their blood. They would still like to come back to the farm. I'd hate to see them get discouraged. It'll turn around. Any of them that can hang in there. I think we're going to be alright."

For now, as far as dairying, he adds, "It's a way of life. And it's my life."

photo by Chuck Blake

**Streeter siblings, from left, Wendell Streeter, Mary Streeter Merz, Eunice Streeter Randall, Irene Streeter Franklin, Eva Streeter Nelson, and Ernest Streeter.**

## "Anything and Everything" at Streeter's Store

### September 6, 1983

*Streeter's and other general stores have long been institutions in our small towns, where people traded with folks they knew. These were retailers who sold practically everything in an era before commercialism began consuming people, before shopping became a pastime unto itself. These were gathering places where you met neighbors, where you bought what you truly needed from people you knew, from traders you trusted. After Streeter's closed in 2006, an organic pizza shop took its place, and a new Dollar General chain store opened about a mile down the road.*

———

A penny buys you a piece of licorice, $47,000 buys you a Massey-Ferguson 140-horsepower tractor.

Streeter's Store in Bernardston has it all.

"If we haven't got it, it can't be too important," says Ernie Streeter, business president and part owner with his four brothers, as many sisters, and two or three nieces and nephews for good measure.

"It works out because everybody is boss," quips sister Eva May Streeter Nelson. "We all work here, some more than others."

But Streeter's—also known as Bernardston Auto Exchange—is more of a family affair than just the roughly twenty "nieces, nephews, outlaws, and in-laws" who pump gas and kerosene, scoop ice cream, and perform other jobs around Franklin County's biggest little store.

In the more than fifty years of business on Route 10, the general store closed only one day. That was in 1957 for the funeral of business owner and the Streeters' father, Harold D. Streeter.

It was a fitting closing. Harold, who opened the business in his house around 1917, was the ultimate Yankee trader, "a salesman who was hard to shake," in the words of his daughter, Eva May.

Bernardston's first gasoline dealer, he kept his fuel in a barrel in his barn, pumped it by hand, and delivered it by horse and buggy, says brother Wendell Streeter.

Stories abound about Harold Streeter's ability to sell anything and everything, including radios, cars, real estate, and appliances.

Greenfield grocer Frank "Bud" Foster, whose wife, June, is Streeter's niece, tells how he was awakened at five or six o'clock one Sunday morning by the master merchant trying to sell him a new 1949 Ford station wagon.

"But I don't want to buy a car," Foster told him. After a while, the reluctant customer agreed to test drive the car on his way to church. When he brought it back and told his uncle-in-law, "It's nice, but I still don't want it," Streeter surprised him.

"It's too late. I've already sold your old one."

Ernie recalls, "He traded for anything. Donkeys, anything."

## Finding It All

You want toys? They've got toys.

You want groceries? There's an entire grocery department.

You want tires? Veterinary supplies? Ammunition, meat, hardware? It's all there, somewhere.

"This building's been full ever since it's been built," says Ernie. Through the years, customers "came for a hell of a lot of stuff that we did have . . . but couldn't find."

In the old days, Streeter's sold pickles, sugar, crackers, and peanut butter from barrels. For twenty years, Streeter's sold milking machines—twenty-five hundred of them—to farmers. Now, as dairy farmers around the region have thinned out, it just sells parts for them.

There was a time, too, when a barber shop was attached to the store and when Streeter's sold cordwood as well.

"In 1933, we sold seventeen hundred cord of wood," recalls Wendell. "And we'd deliver to Turners Falls, to Greenfield, to Millers Falls for five dollars and seven dollars a cord. And that was one man using a crosscut saw and ax."

Sister Eunice Streeter Randall says she appreciates having oil heat in the store now and remembers having to throw logs into the furnace.

The Streeters once had their own slaughterhouse where Harold's brother Herman slaughtered animals. Now the Streeters butcher meat that's been slaughtered elsewhere.

Wendell, Eunice, and the others remember plucking the feathers off chickens like the two thousand birds their father bought one time during World War II and sold during a ten-week period.

What people won't find at Streeter's but reportedly ask for fifteen or twenty times a day during summer is beer.

"We get asked more and more for beer every year," says Wendell. "We never did, and we never will. We weren't brought up to sell booze. We were brought up strict Methodists, and our parents taught us we'd go straight to hell in a handbasket if we did."

Still, there's enough other merchandise on the two-thousand-square-foot main floor to keep any Franklin County shopper busy browsing.

Among its myriad other items, Streeter's sells Teddy bears made by Ernie's wife and hand-smocked dresses made by one of the daughters-in-law. Maple syrup, which Ernie's son Ron makes in Leyden, sells in the store at the rate of two hundred gallons a year, by Wendell's reckoning.

Streeter's "has meant a lot of different things to different people," says Eunice. Some people say they've been all over, looking for a certain item. They ask, 'Do you have it?' Usually, we do."

The youngest of the Streeter siblings, Eunice remembers when she was a little girl coming home from school to scoop ice cream at her family's store.

"But what really used to intrigue me," she recalls, "was the tobacco cutter. We used to cut little plugs of chewing tobacco."

From behind the wooden counter, she looks at brother Wendell.

"Whatever happened to our tobacco cutter?"

"It's upstairs, "he tells her, as if the answer were obvious.

In the store's attic, up a narrow flight of wooden stairs—"Don't knock your head over here," advises Wendell as he leads a visitor up— are rakes, aluminum garbage cans, stovepipe, window glass, an array of fan belts, and other assorted hardware items.

Downstairs, in space that used to be rented for state highway trucks and town fire trucks, tractors and autos are repaired by five mechanics. There's also a hydraulic drill and a lathe to do machine work.

As if three immense floors are not enough, Streeter's also has a trailer parked back where they keep barbed wire, twine, "and lots of things we don't seem to have room for in the building," as Wendell puts it.

As part of the auto-repair business—Bernardston Auto Exchange has two wreckers, one car carrier and a twenty-four-hour towing service.

A half dozen tractors are parked opposite the store across the street in front of brother Jamie's house. Farther down South Street, behind the garage, is other farm equipment which Ernie says hasn't been selling well in recent years.

That, says Wendell, is where diversification pays off for the family business.

### Capitalizing . . . or Not

With a little spit, polish, and slick advertising, Streeter's could capitalize on the potential tourist trade. Even more than the postcards and Streeter's T-shirts the store sells, the emporium just off the interstate highway, after all, could cash in on its down-home, country-store image as stores in Williamsburg, Guilford, Vermont, and other places have done.

The quintessential Yankee family could, but the Streeters don't want to.

"You get to thinking about what to change," says Eunice, "and then someone comes in and tells you how he loves your good old wooden floors. We had a man come in who says he graduated from

135

nearby Mount Hermon School and how thrilled he was to come back here and find everything just the same."

Business nowadays splits almost evenly among hardware, farm equipment and repairs, and gasoline and car repairs.

Among customers, there are regulars—local farm families with three hundred or four hundred active Streeter's charge accounts, Wendell reckons.

"I've got one family I can tell you that I've sold to for six generations."

There are other regulars, too—tourists who stop in each summer on their way going to and returning from Vermont or New Hampshire. The state line is just a few miles up the road, after all.

Store hours are daily from 7:30 in the morning until at least 6:30 in the evening, and some nights until 9, but there were years, Ernie recalls, when it was open from 7 until 11.

"The business hasn't grown much," he offers with typical dry humor, "but it has grown more confusing."

Some years, Ernie adds, business even approached the million-dollar mark, making it the biggest little store around.

"We aren't any closer to being broke than we were twenty-five or thirty years ago. But we're just as close."

**Paul Winter**

# "Make Room for the Immensities!"

## August 27, 2008

*"How long has it been since you've had a good howl?"* saxophonist
*Paul Winter typically asked at his concerts. The question came after*

*he played his legendary tune "Wolf Eyes" to the accompaniment of recorded wolf howls—an implicit invitation for the audience to let loose their primal natures. His music, which connects us with nature and with the world's rhythms, certainly spoke to me, and I was delighted to interview him on a couple of occasions.*

———

Six-time Grammy Award winner Paul Winter is known for mimicking the cries of wolves, whales, and birds with his soprano saxophone and incorporating them into his music along with the recorded animal wailing. But he's never before been known to incorporate the lowing of cows—at least not until.

Winter, about to perform a pair of benefit concerts for Vermont's Strolling of the Heifers parade in Brattleboro, may just surprise the audiences with the plaintive lowing of cattle on his own horn. In any case, calling people's attention to caring for all creatures huge and small is nothing new for him.

For decades an explorer of the world's musical traditions and a Pied Piper celebrating "creatures and cultures of the whole earth," Winter also embraces wonder of the environment as a big part of his eclectic blend of sounds wild and worldly.

"The whole journey has been one of gradual expansion of the idea of community and a sense of home," says Winter. The musician-composer-bandleader, 70, has been playing one musical instrument or another since the age of three. "That sense of home expands to embrace the whole planet."

And Winter, whose far-reaching musical embrace has both anticipated and soared beyond conventional labels like New Age and world music, isn't just talking about humans.

Maybe the most prescient criticism of Winter came from a conductor when Winter was a first-grade drum-playing applicant trying out for the Baker School Orchestra in Altoona, Pennsylvania: "He plays where he shouldn't."

## Playing Outside the Box

Winter went on to learn piano and clarinet, then playing saxophone in a variety of jazz bands before leading a jazz sextet that won a Columbia Records contract in 1961 and was invited the following year as the first-ever jazz group to play at the White House. He helped pioneer an exploration of Brazilian music in the early 1960s with his album "Jazz Meets the Bossa Nova" and in 1967 formed the groundbreaking Paul Winter Consort.

One year later, he discovered a recording of humpback whales, and three years after that, the consort's *Road* album was flown by astronauts aboard Apollo 15 to the moon. They named two newly-discovered craters there for Winter's songs "Icarius" and "Ghost Beads."

Paul Winter played for whales as part of a 1973 Greenpeace expedition in the North Pacific. His 1984 *Concert for the Earth* was the first jazz album ever recorded in the United Nations, as part of its official World Environment Day observance. The Paul Winter Consort has also recorded at the Grand Canyon, played a 1985 concert in San Francisco together with a chorus singing simultaneously in Moscow, and has since 1980 been artist in residence at New York's Cathedral of St. John the Divine. There the consort has performed annual broadcast celebrations for the winter and summer solstice as well as an annual *Earth Mass* on the Feast of St. Francis.

There are so many firsts for Winter, in fact, with recording expeditions to thirty-six countries and wilderness areas on six continents, that it's hard to imagine him playing the down-to-earth role of father of two young daughters back home in western Connecticut.

"It's as if music has led me on this amazing magic carpet to a journey into life and the world," says Winter, whose music is a mesmerizing mix of African and Arabic rhythms, mammal and bird calls, and all the world's instruments including voice. "It just keeps getting better."

Becoming a parent late in life "has opened me to a whole new realm of miracles, challenges and deep commitments," including a desire to stay closer to home even as his latest musical project has taken him to far-flung recording venues like Japan and Brazil.

That four-year project *Flyways* is a typical Winteresque visionary melding of twenty world cultures and environmental awareness: a musical celebration of the great bird migrations from Africa to the Middle East, Asia, and back, chronicling long avian journeys by recording with indigenous musicians around the world.

Along the way, the connections that Winter makes with different cultures, with different species, and with the music itself are part of a spiritual connection.

"For me, the music is the spirituality," Winter says. "It transcends explanation or definition. For me, music has always been by far and away the most nourishing realm. It keeps reawakening the sense of relatedness to a larger perspective, a larger community."

## "Immensities" of Winter

When he's been on the road and has missed playing his sax for a morning or two, it's felt to Winter that he's lost not only his "musical compass" but his moral center as well, as if getting tossed in a sea of stresses and losing sight of his beacon. "Make room for the immensities!" he says. "Don't get caught up with trivialities."

Winter's musical journeys, which began with a six-month US State Department tour of twenty-three Latin American countries in 1966, have also brought home for him the stark reality of how native musical traditions are threatened even as world music has become another reality of a shrinking planet.

"Endangered cultures are as much the focus of this as endangered species and habitat, "he says. "I hope bringing the magic of the traditions of the world will awaken a broader sense of concern among people to conserve the treasure that's being lost."

He fears, too, for "the traditions of music we love and revere in an age of monoculture and mass media. I hear the things my daughter listens to on her iPod, and I think, 'Are there any melodies any more?'"

Yet he keeps in perspective the likelihood that parents have always disapproved of the music listened to by their children. Still, "The area where I feel the most optimism is with the voices of the wild creatures."

All kids seem fascinated at hearing the voices of whales and wolves. Winter believes such primal sounds strongly recall "a certain deep archetypal dimension of our species's memory going back hundreds of thousands of years, the vast majority of which was spent living in community with wild creatures. I have no idea if my music will connect with teenagers, but I'm optimistic about my four-year-old and other kids who haven't been acculturated by media."

In founding the Living Music recording label in the late 1970s, Winter's intention was "to strive towards timeless music, to record in natural acoustic spaces, like stone canyons or the loft of a barn and to create a catalogue that would embrace the vital traditions of music we revere, from Bach to Africa, and cello to wolves."

## Cathedrals and Heifers

Through it all, Winter sees a connection between the spiritual breadth of music and the ecological.

"These are traditions deep in human heritage, people living on the land and from the land," Winter says. "If people can no longer do that, it will be an irreplaceable loss for humanity."

Everything comes together always for Paul Winter. But especially gratifying are the twice-annual solstice celebrations at the Manhattan cathedral, where a cross-section of generations find common ground in that cavernous space.

His *Earth Mass* there each spring since 1981 even includes an invitation for people to bring along their pets to celebrate the connection of all earth's creatures.

Winter's voice begins almost to glow as he describes the grand interspecies procession that's included an elephant, a camel, a llama, chimpanzees, ferrets, a twelve-foot boa constrictor wrapped around one celebrant's neck, and more.

"Under all the layers of sophistication, we're all connected in the realm of the animal world. For me, it's profoundly encouraging when that memory is tapped. For me, that's the meaning of the word sacred."

photo by Paul Franz

**Ethan Schweitzer-Gaslin**
## Tour de Crème

### July 14, 2007

*With a Howard Johnson's practically in the backyard of my childhood home, ice cream has always had a special place in my heart. It seemed obvious that I needed a candid, hyperarticulate, exuberant soulmate in scoops to keep me from going overboard as I undertook my magnum ice cream opus. How else to eloquently articulate the joys of this simple frozen confection? I've known Ethan since before he was born. The Recorder accompanied the article with photos of Ethan interpreting an ice cream cone in dance, since he was a budding ballet dancer. He's since gone on to dance with Ballet Idaho.*

"Let the lamp affix its beam.
The only emperor is the emperor of ice cream."

—Wallace Stevens

When my editor assigned me to "Find the best ice cream in all of Franklin County," I was sure I'd died and gone to heaven. Given my heart condition, I realized, that could just happen. Maybe I need to double my Lipitor regimen, just in case.

Besides, *best* sometimes is a matter of what's handy and what you're up for.

For help, I enlisted Ethan Schweitzer-Gaslin—a thirteen-year-old buddy I'd known since he was a gleam in his mother's eye who would surely delight in spending his first week of summer vacation as my young ice cream man.

So we fasten our seatbelts and loosen our belts for the Tour de Crème, a two-day exploration of fifteen different local parlors extraordinaire.

### Day 1: Takeoff!

There are so many ice-cream places from Harper's Package Store to Brad's Place in Greenfield to Jerry's Place in South Deerfield that it's bewildering to know where to begin. But Ethan begins with a confession, "I love ice cream almost as much as flying in an airplane."

So what better takeoff point than across from Turners Falls Airport at The Country Creemee? Fasten those seatbelts again. The choices there seem staggering: vanilla and pistachio frozen yogurt and watermelon as the special soft-serve flavor. Beyond the creamy clouds, the creemee, apart from its too many *E*s, is even dishing out seven snow-cone flavors, including bubble gum and grape.

We start simply with soft vanilla ice cream in a dish.

My precocious partner in crème immediately enthuses, "This is fabulous! You can almost taste the flavor of fresh cream in there. It's not too sugary, but it's satisfying if you have a sweet tooth."

"Wow," I think, more bowled over by Ethan's five-star critique than by the soft serve we're sampling.

Ethan, who's just finished seventh grade at Greenfield Center School, is still bubbling as we drive off: "It was a simple, pure ice cream that had that innocent taste of a summer day when you're sitting around eating that little bite."

With my loquacious pal dressed in off-white shorts, sandals, and a blue Amherst Ballet T-shirt, we continue prowling for our just desserts by heading toward Yelena's Soft Serve on Turners Falls Road. After cleansing the palate, of course.

The simple, white-block stand has more than thirty varieties of soft-serve and maybe twenty-plus varieties of the hard stuff. Suddenly, we are so lost in a sea of selections that the patient man at the window wonders if we're ever going to settle on something before it all begins melting.

## Like, a Gazillion Flavors!

"There's, like, a gazillion flavors!" proclaims Ethan. "I suppose in some ways, it will keep you coming back for more."

We settle in for a German chocolate soft-serve cone, easily bypassing the month's special flavors: bubble gum, eggnog, cotton candy, apple pie, pineapple, and custard.

Ethan, who visited Germany last year with his parents, once again rises to the occasion: "This doesn't taste like the chocolate I had in Germany, but I don't think that's necessarily the intention. It's very coffee-y but has a much more dense flavor."

The kindercritic tells me the concoction was reminiscent of chocolate he ate in Bavaria, yet it has a "sleek, chic" flavor. Meanwhile, brown goop begins dripping from his cone as we wait for our photographer to arrive. "This isn't going to be fit to photograph," Ethan cautions.

Then, before you can say "hot fudge," we head off to the Shady Glen, where we choose chocolate chip from a half dozen flavors of Snow's Ice Cream—the first of many stops where we find the hard, Greenfield-made brand and its upscale premium sister, Bart's.

Chocolate chip is a favorite of mine, so I await my sidekick's in-depth verdict.

"This is a very grainy ice cream," comes Ethan's critique after he swirls a mouthful around that golden tongue like vintage Merlot. "At the same time, I feel like every individual grain in this ice cream is like an exploding pocket of flavor that just bursts in your mouth. It changes from second to second. Or probably doesn't, but it seems to."

Yikes. I want this young maven to tell it like it is, and I think he's channeling Ben and Jerry.

## Keep You Interested

The Dynamic Dairy Duo crosses the mighty Connecticut River for the Wagon Wheel Drive-In Restaurant on Route 2 in Gill. There, we select a dish of lemon sorbet from a list of Bart's Homemade flavors.

"It's hard to taste much but the lemon," Ethan tells me, "but you can certainly taste that very strongly, and I think it's a very good thing. I imagine it would be very refreshing on a scorching day or when it's humid out. It's not too complicated, but it's enough to keep you interested, enough to keep your mouth wanting more, to keep your taste buds wanting to explore it."

We are already halfway out of town with Ethan still waxing poetic and me watching what look like clouds of vanilla and ominous chocolate overhead. Cows dot the hillside at Justadream Farm to remind us that, sorbet aside, dairy is what this two-day adventure is all about.

"That makes you want to eat ice cream!" Ethan heralds, as he takes note of the bovine-dotted landscape.

We pull into the Northfield Creamie where the choices are, once again, daunting (Do we want a purple Barney dip? A green Celtics dip?). We select a chocolate-dipped vanilla cone.

"The chocolate dip really does it well, sort of like putting on a fancy suit. It adds a nice other element to it: it's very crisp. In fact, the whole flavor is very crisp and clean, straightforward, if you know what I mean," Ethan observes.

I don't, but we drive off toward Bernardston anyway.

"I thought I could eat ice cream all day, but it's not at all easy," Ethan admits.

At Town Line Creamies—noted on its sign as TLC, a name that amuses Ethan—we look over a list of Gifford's Ice Cream flavors like Maine Birch Bark, Black Raspberry Bugaboo Fudge, and Blue-Ribbon Strawberry. We pass up soft-serve and order a hard-chocolate cone.

"It's refreshingly dry," Ethan tells me. "It's as close as you can get to the polar opposite of Snow's."

I believe our little la leche lad is beginning to show signs of overdose. But we press on, all the way to West County.

"This has a lovely old charm!" says Ethan as we enter Baker Pharmacy in Shelburne Falls and sit down at its blast-from-the-past soda fountain for a dish of Snow's Chocolate Zig-Zag.

"It's really quite exceptional. Just one of those things in life that makes you say, 'Mmmm,'" Ethan confides. "Sort of a little time machine that whisks me right back to the nineteenth century."

Across the Iron Bridge at McCusker's Market, I was under the delusion they still sell OatsCrème, a dairy-free soft-serve product that I figured could be a welcome change of pace. We find it's long gone but we're offered Bart's raspberry-coconut-heavy Three Geeks and a Redhead. Yet, since Ethan doesn't like coconut, we select Moose Tracks, instead.

## Fruity, Light, and Fairly Simple

Ethan tells me, "This tastes very similar to Chocolate Zig-Zag, but the chocolate in this is very different. The other one had a very homey, warm comfortable feeling. This one is a very exciting flavor."

There's one more stop on the Buckland side of the river—Christopher's, formerly Josie's, where we get a raspberry soft-serve frozen yogurt cone. Ethan finds it "fruity, light, and fairly simple."

As we head further west to what we believe will be the last stop of our first day of touring, my co-connoisseur confesses, "I'm dying to eat as little ice cream as possible for the rest of my life."

At Curtis Country Store in Charlemont, my effusive sidekick announces, a moment after walking in, "It's amazing in here: it's the middle of June, and it smells like sugaring season."

With that down-home observation as prelude, we order a dish of Bart's Mudpie frozen yogurt with chocolate sprinkles. which Ethan declares has "a very unique flavor, like the opposite of the coffee spectrum from the German chocolate we had."

My eyes are riveted on a sign announcing that the store sells Charlemont's Own Homemade Ice Cream in pints and quarts. And, as I suspect, store owner John Miller makes it at his nearby Farm at Mine Brook. So why not visit?

Within five minutes, we're at Miller's Mountain Road hideaway. Miller, who is said to also scoop his homemade ice cream there, is just about to milk his Jerseys. But we got to sample some of his Native Blueberry flavor made with berries handpicked by his mother. We also checked out Honey Roasted Peanut Butter Swirl.

"I can't get away from the fact that people want sweet and gooey," says Miller, who's just begun making his sixteen-percent butterfat ice cream in small batches and selling it at the store and the farm. He's also selling a Very Vanilla flavor and has made a Blueberry Cheesecake ice cream with his own goat's milk chèvre as one of the ingredients.

Miller's Jersey Maid is a small-batch super-premium ice cream whose sixteen-percent butterfat creaminess and freshness stand out as "out of this world," to quote my junior partner.

And as we finish off our first ninety-six-mile tour leg, Ethan becomes bullish on the dairy treat once more.

"This is the perfect topper of the day!" he declares. "That just sort of says Western Mass. We saw the guy about to milk the cows. And his mother grows the blueberries and personally handpicks them. And personally brings them to him! And he personally makes the ice cream from the milk from his cows!"

In fact, as we head back toward Greenfield, my creamy companion reflects on "the ideal ice-cream experience":

"We sit in the barn with the cows and maybe sleep with the cows and wake up in the morning and help the person milk cows or maybe watch him milk and make the cream and churn it with the ice. And we eat it, not even in a bowl, but with a scoop into your mouth."

"Mmm," I say, echoing the cows that had made the day's delights possible.

## Day 2: I Scream: More?

Day 1 was a hard act to follow, so Day 2 begins at Snow's Ice Cream Company in Greenfield for a quick Wonka-esque tour to plumb the inner mysteries of concocting frozen delights.

Co-owner Gary Schaefer, who's been making Bart's Homemade since 1978 and five years later bought the Snow's brand and School Street factory, leads us past the continuous ice-cream freezer that workers use to make Snow's chocolate ice cream. We head into the cooler, where three-hundred-gallon bags of mix—in plain and chocolate flavors— wait to be pumped into tanks to be made into ice cream.

The name Tommy is autographed on the vintage 1950s equipment left there by former ice-cream maker Tommy Snow himself. Ethan will tell me later, "I expected the factory to be big and booming and really industrial. But it's not. It's nice and small . . . and like a family."

The chocolate ice cream Schaefer hands Ethan is a sample. It resembles more the soft-serve than the hard product it would become and is one of between six and nine flavors being made in any given day.

"Mmmm! Oh, my goodness!" rhapsodizes the young critic. "That's some of the best chocolate ice cream I've ever had!"

Schaefer shows off the Jack the Rippler machine, which can twirl in liquid ingredients, and the Big Bubba device, which can add solid candies and nuts. He tells us 300 gallons of mix will make either 600 gallons of 12-percent butterfat Snow's or 360 gallons of 16-percent Bart's Ice Cream.

After emerging from the fifteen-degree hardening room, where an overnight stay makes ice cream rock-hard, we get the scoop on Bart's newest flavors—Mass Mocha, Caramel Moose Trails, and Deep Purple Cow—as well as the super-premium soft-serve Frozen Custard he's just introduced at the Bart's parlor on Main Street in Greenfield. The custard has eleven-percent butterfat instead of the five to ten percent for regular soft-serve along with egg yolks and more milk solids. It's popular in the Midwest and in New York. Schaefer hopes it will raise eyebrows here as well.

So we head over to the Bart's parlor on Main Street, where owner Alan Sax proudly holds a one-ounce cone of French vanilla—you buy ice cream by the ounce there—perpendicular to the floor to demonstrate how stable it is. In addition to a whole lot of Bart's and Snow's hard ice creams and sorbets, there's also Double Dutch Chocolate nonfat frozen yogurt to keep dieters from sinning. But Sax boasts that the frozen custard is "a glorious thing not known in this area: eggier and more decadent."

"Ooooo! That's a breed of its own," wails Ethan. "I could never get enough of that. My tongue keeps hoping it will be finding more."

He cleanses his young palate with water as we drive to Friendly's. There, a request for a Wattamelon Roll cone—a seasonal concoction I remember as having chocolate-chip "seeds" and a lemon-lime rind—is met with a blank stare from the young take-out window attendant. So, instead, we settle for a cup of watermelon sherbet.

"That's very refreshing," remarks Ethan. "It reminds me of a late-night club in uptown Manhattan."

Hmm. I do a double take, reminding myself that this is a thirteen-year-old kid from the wilds of bucolic Montague. He adds, "It's very light and happy, and it pops in your mouth. And it's the color of bright hot pink markers you'd find in a classroom."

At Richardson's Candy Kitchen in Deerfield, which scoops out nine flavors of Herrell's Ice Cream, we choose a cup of Malted Vanilla, and Ethan is beside himself.

"It's splendid!" he raves. "It tastes like you're eating malted-milk balls. That's so complex with flavors piled on top of each other. The cream tastes like it's flowing in your mouth. I wonder what the cows would think of this? It's like being in an old country store."

Next, we're off to 5J Creamee at Jim Pasiecnik's Whately farmstand for a strawberry sundae made with fresh strawberries picked a few hundred feet from the take-out window.

"We're going to have to eat more than a few bites of this," Ethan recommends as it's prepared. He's overheard by curious bystanders unaware that we've been sampling nibbles of ice cream for hours.

"That's fabulous!" he exclaims as he works his way past the whipped cream and into the sundae itself.

"The strawberries add a whole other element. The ice cream is the catalyst for the juicy syrup, which provides a cushion on the bottom and enriches the different layers. This is fun, and it's hard to stop eating!"

But stop we must, for it's time to head west to the Ashfield Hardware Store. There, amid the hammers and nails, lightbulbs and pails, Ashfielders in the know get their ice cream scooped.

Co-owner Laura Bessette holds a scoop as she stands by a cooler with a few flavors of Snow's ice cream and a sign that says *In Ice Cream We Trust*. It also announces that cones are just a dollar—or fifty cents for kids' sizes. If children bring in two golf balls from the course across the street, they get a free cone.

"We wanted the spirit of good will and ice cream to prevail. A lot of kids are hard up for cash," she tells us, as she hands Ethan a small Mudpie cone. "We think it's important they be able to find an affordable treat."

## Make Ice Cream, Not War

On our way out of the store, Bessette shows us a posted photo of happy kids—the annual visit to the store by Ashfield preschoolers learning about commerce and community: ice-cream ambassadors.

Ethan tells me he likes that Mudpie better than the one we had earlier, and I can't help but wonder whether it was a reaction to the good vibes in the place.

Sure enough, he observes, "It's comforting to know that there is still someplace where ice cream still costs fifty cents so kids can come in and have an affordable treat and that kids can feel really special about getting ice cream. They can collect golf balls and buy ice cream with golf balls. What a novel concept. It's really nice to know that they're in it to make people happy, which is how people should behave."

I'm in awe: into his thirteen-year-old mouth goes a taste of ice cream and out comes wisdom.

"Instead of having wars, we should eat ice cream together," Ethan adds.

By then, we're passing Creamery Road, which Ethan points out in an offhanded way is "very fitting."

I'm beginning to imagine the cows in the field by the side of the road with signs that say, Eat More Ice Cream, which probably means we've both eaten too much of it.

At Baker's Country Store in Conway, further along Route 116, Ethan notes the attractive display of produce outside, and I notice two tables of regulars seated in front of shelves of canned goods. But for a scoop of Snow's ice cream—we choose coffee flavor—we're led into a side parlor.

"This is a lovely place," Ethan tells me, as he nibbles some ice cream and we walk along the South River back toward the car. "Rural Franklin County is what we're exploring with this ice-cream tour. This is probably one of the last places where you can still listen to the birds sing and eat a good cone."

Our final stop is Sugar Loaf Frostee in Sunderland, where you can order everything from hamburgers and fries to Bomb Pops and Flurries. We each order a vanilla creamee. Our last.

"It makes you smile," says Ethan, before correcting himself. "It makes ONE smile when you eat it. It is frosty but smooth—frostee cream! This isn't ice cream, This is frostee cream."

As we wander off reflecting on our crème de la crème experience, I ask Ethan what he's learned from our edible adventure.

"Hmmm. That's a very good question. I learned you really can eat too much ice cream. You can, and do, and in our case did have too much ice cream."

But then Ethan tops his reply, à la mode: "Sometimes it's not the ice cream that makes the memory sweet but the people and places where you had it—the atmosphere and the surroundings, and everybody there puts a bit of themselves into the ice cream. It will taste different, because different people loved it in different ways."

Hail, Ethan, Emperor of Ice Cream!

# With Gratitude . . .

Creating this volume has served as a reminder not just of those people who helped me realize this collection of articles, but the people who've assisted through the years in making my work possible. I express my deep appreciation to

- all of my editors at the *Recorder* through the years for their dedication to quality journalism in Franklin County
- Marcia Gagliardi of Haley's for her encouragement, editing and painstakingly following through
- Becky (the Clark matriarch) Clark for her pastel artwork for the cover and Lindy Whiton for her author's photo
- B. J. Roche for contributing her thoughtful foreword
- photographers Paul Franz, Peter MacDonald. and posthumously, Chuck Blake, with whom I collaborated over the years and whose photographs complement the stories. And Steven Rodman, Rami Efal, Artemis Joukowsky, and all those who who assisted me in tracking down and securing the rights to other photos accompanying these stories
- my wife, Susan, for her critical support, invaluable suggestions, and careful review of the manuscript
- the people of Franklin County and its surroundings who have given and continue to provide me with so much to appreciate and write about

photo by Lindy Whiton

**Richie Davis**

# About the Author

Richie Davis won more than thirty-five regional news and
featurewriting awards as a reporter and editor for more than forty
years at The Recorder of Greenfield in western Massachusetts.
Engaging environmental, political, and societal issues, he wrote dozens
of in-depth series on topics ranging from nuclear power and the
aging population to high-tech cottage industries. He won a Pulitzer
Center on Crisis Reporting grant for coverage of an effort to foster
cross-cultural dialogue. But among his favorite works have been
profiles of intriguing, ordinary people.

He blogs at his website, RichieDavis.net

# Colophon

Text for *Good Will & Ice Cream* is set in Sabon, an old-style serif typeface and effectively a Garamond revival designed between 1964 and 1967 by the Germanborn typographer and designer Jan Tschichold (1902–1974). The Linotype, Monotype, and Stempel type foundries jointly released Sabon in 1967. Tschichold based the design of the roman on types by Claude Garamond (c. 1480–1561), particularly a specimen printed by the Frankfurt printer Konrad Berner. Berner had married the widow of a fellow printer Jacques Sabon, the source of the face's name, who had bought some of Garamond's type after his death. Italics are based on types designed by a contemporary of Garamond's, Robert Granjon. Titles and captions are set in News Gothic, a realist sans-serif typeface dated to 1908, designed by Morris Fuller Benton, and released by his employer American Type Founders. News Gothic is similar in proportion and structure to Franklin Gothic, also designed by Benton, but lighter.

Inner Landscapes
*True Tales from Extraordinary Lives*
RICHIE DAVIS

forty years of writing in *The Recorder*
of western Massachusetts

photos by Paul Franz

- an inner-city teen bonds with a ninety-two-year-old farmer who's always lived off the land
- ready to resume life together and renew their vows, a married couple reunites after five years of separation, but the attacks of September 11, 2001 interfere
- a lifelong polio victim, confined for decades, soars by writing haiku
- two veteran folk musicians join forces to rediscover the power of writing and sharing music in the face of memory loss.

an intimate and engaging look at an unspoiled
fascinating slice of uncommon people
who care for the land and each other.

*Inner Landscapes* opens up a beneath-the-surface glimpse of
life off the beaten path.

*Inner Landscapes* tells down-to-earth stories of farmers, of thoughtful, hardscrabble women and men, of refugees from towns now underwater, of people whose lives have been altered by dementia and newfound passions as first told in the pages of the *Recorder* of Greenfield, Massachusetts.

" . . . a beautiful new book, and a moving book . . . an extraordinary book."
—Bill Newman
WHMP, Northampton

available online at richiedavis.net

ISBN 978-1-948380-33-1 • $14.95

Haley's • Athol, Massachusetts